SMALL
BUSINESS
PRIMER

SMALL
BUSINESS
PRIMER
How to
BUY
SELL &
EVALUATE
a Business

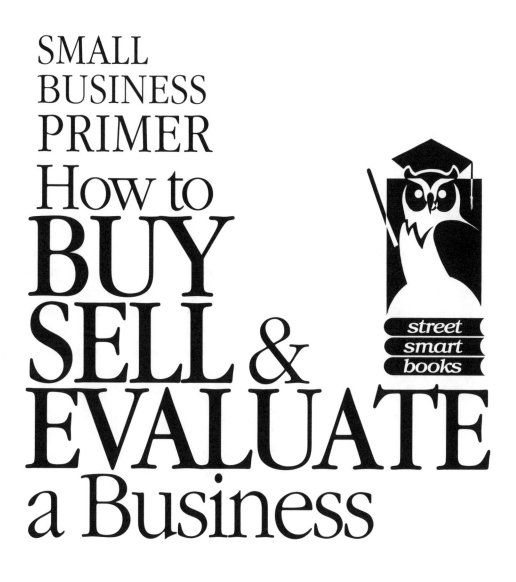

street
smart
books

Samuel S. Tuttle, CCIM
My "Seminar-in-a-Book"

streetsmartbooks Middletown, Delaware

Small Business Primer: How To Buy, Sell, and Evaluate a Business by Samuel S. Tuttle, CCIM

Published by streetsmartbooks, LLC. For information, visit www.streetsmartbooks.com or write to: streetsmartbooks, LLC, P.O. Box 2, Middletown, DE 19709-0002.

Notice: This publication contains the opinions and ideas of its author. It is intended to provide helpful and informative material on the subject matters covered. It is sold with the understanding that the author and publisher are not engaged in rendering professional services in this book. If the reader requires personal assistance or advice, a competent professional should be consulted. This book is offered without guarantee on the part of the author or streetsmartbooks, LLC. The author and streetsmartbooks, LLC, specifically disclaim any responsibility for any liability, loss, or risk, personal or otherwise, which is incurred as a consequence, directly or indirectly, of the use and/or application of any of the contents of this book.

Cover and Interior Design by Pneuma Books: Complete Publisher's Services
Visit www.pneumadesign.com/books/info for more information.
streetsmartbooks logo designed by Delaware Design Co. delarwaredesign@aol.com

Library of Congress Cataloging-in-Publication Data
Tuttle, Samuel S.
 Small business primer : how to buy, sell & evaluate a business / Samuel S. Tuttle. — 1st ed.
 p. cm.
 Includes index.
 LCCN: 2001117100
 ISBN: 0-9709466-0-0
 1. Small business—United States—Purchasing. 2. Sale of small businesses—United States. I. Title.
 HD2346.U5T88 2002   658.02'2
                QBI101-200425

Printed in the United States of America by Thomson Shore, Dexter, MI
10 09 08 07 06 05 04 03 02 01   10 09 08 07 06 05 04 03 02 01

...from the Author

Congratulations on being a part of the world of small business — the backbone of the American economy! For maximum impact we suggest you read the entire book through, then take one chapter at a time and complete the checklist at the end of the chapter. Take some time for reflective thought. Discuss the subject matter with those who may become involved with your business venture and with those whose opinions you value.

Small Business Primer may give you different perspectives when you change from buyer to seller or when you need to determine your business's value. Keep the book in your library and refer to it when needed.

The most important lesson you can take from this book is "Make Your Own Decisions". Get all the information. Investigate thoroughly. Solicit advice and opinions from others. But make your own decisions.

Good luck in the world of small business. May you achieve your highest goal.

—Samuel S. Tuttle, CCIM

Contents

List of Chapter Topics

- Small Business Development Centers
- SBA's Entrepreneurial Development Program
- Business Information Centers
- Bankers
- Accountants
- Better Business Bureaus
- Chambers of Commerce
- Universities' Schools of Business
- Trade Associations/Journals
- Business People
- Service Clubs
- Internet
- Clients
- Customers
- Friends (Even Relatives)

Appendix
- Find a CCIM
- Business Forms
- Software and Publications
- Other Information Sources
- Websites

Acknowledgments

Ten years in the making, *Small Business Primer* is not a work that I could have accomplished alone. I need to thank all of you who attended my seminars over the years, and who gave valuable input about what kinds of information you needed. Thanks to all of my customers and clients who have trusted my advice, causing me to rise to the occasion and find new and better ways to be diligent in my practice. Thanks to Norm Hatter, Paul Roessel, Rob Bostick, Gene Cochrane, Dave Harris, and Pete Kelso for their input and ideas. Special thanks to Dave Smith and Rob Webster for their thorough editing of my manuscript. A special thanks to Kyle Stevenson, Executive Vice President of Business Loan Express, for his valuable input on the chapter on financing. Thanks to those who prefer to remain my unsung heroes.

As an author, I need to thank my family for their tolerance, encouragement, and support throughout the writing of this book. That would be my wife, Sandy, whose encouragement drove me to completion, and my sister, Dee Hill, whose suggestions and honest criticisms made the book better than I could have done by myself.

Special thanks to Brian and Nina Taylor of Pneuma Books whose wonderfully creative minds turned my manuscript into this professional publication. Their ideas and criticisms were freely exchanged, and their talent speaks for itself.

The author welcomes comments and criticisms from all readers. Buying, selling, or evaluating a small business is not a science — it is truly an art. Comments may be e-mailed to author@streetsmartbooks.com, or sent from our website: http//www.streetsmartbooks.com.

—Samuel S. Tuttle, CCIM

Foreword
by Richard Dodson

This book is a real eye-opener. I have known the author for about eight years through our business brokerage and commercial real estate networks and have always been impressed with his willingness to share tips and techniques with anyone in need. He is one of the best problem-solvers and obstacle-overcomers I've ever met. Now, he is offering you a wealth of "streetsmart" knowledge for what it would cost you to spend twenty minutes with him on the clock in his consulting practice. There is no way you could get this volume of critical information from him at an affordable cost, except from this book.

Small Business Primer is packed with insider knowledge and seasoned with over twenty years of experience. There is nothing boring about this book. Not only will it help many buyers and sellers, but I predict it will become the textbook for business brokers across America as well. I know I will be using it in all my classes.

This is not just a book — it is the valuable information you need.

Richard Dodson, CBB, CCS;
President, Dodson & Associates, Inc. — Business Brokerage
President, Mid-Atlantic Business Brokers Association
rwdodson@dc.infi.net

SMALL
BUSINESS
PRIMER

How to
BUY
SELL &
EVALUATE
a Business

Introduction

Over the past twenty years, the author has given seminars to a variety of listeners about the subject at hand. Business professionals. Business Brokers. Real estate agents. Buyers. Sellers. And the curious.

Although there are a few books about the subject available, there does not seem to be a simple primer that combines common sense, tempered with seasoned and experienced guidance to help the buyer and seller, and that helps to empower buyers and sellers to make the difficult decisions they need to be successful. This is such a book.

This book is the first in a series of streetsmartbooks publications. They will be books "from the trenches" written by experienced professionals in their areas of specialization. For more information about the coming series, visit our web site at www.streetsmartbooks.com.

Because it is true that buying, selling, or evaluating a small business is a difficult, fact-based experience, most people tend to approach the task armed only with numbers, facts, and figures. If this approach were correct, then most successful business owners would be accountant-types. This is not the case. The most successful entrepreneurs are those who make good decisions on the gut level — after, of course, getting all the facts needed to make the respective decisions. This book, instead of providing charts and graphs for quick business evaluations, is written to arm you with ideas and concepts to help you develop the senses needed to make good decisions. Numbers will be addressed, but the dangers of using numbers only will also be clearly expressed.

By immersing you in thought patterns and activities necessary to truly understand a business's most critical areas, I plan to prepare you to educate yourself about upcoming decisions. You will find that no one should make your decisions for you. Since you will live or die by your decisions in the business world, never trust anyone to make them for you. You will be directed to use professionals for advice in areas of specialty,

such as law, accounting, real estate, and taxation. But these professionals can only advise you within their areas of competence. You must make your own decisions.

Although scores of legal and administrative bureaus have successfully lobbied to have many laws and regulations passed to control the formulas and contents of number-based representations, these numbers continue to be the prime area where it is easiest to mislead your otherwise sound judgments concerning businesses. If it were possible to buy, sell, or evaluate a small business without using any numbers at all I would be a proponent of the method. It is not. The ability to base your decisions on areas other than numbers (e.g., goals, sentiments, experience, judgments, and common sense) will enhance your probability of making good decisions.

Don't look for lots of charts, graphs, and tables. Although they can be important, there are no genuine comprehensive indexes for this subject matter. The varied aspects of individual businesses preclude any common formula for analysis. Each business area must be considered individually, and you must base your decisions on information gained in each area after thorough investigation. This is what will set you apart from the rest.

Everyone is a first-timer so don't feel overwhelmed. Get excited! Get counsel. There is no substitute for experience, but you have to start somewhere. Remember to use common sense, sharpen your people skills, investigate thoroughly, and listen to counselors with genuine *street smarts*.

As you read this book, remember that buyers need to think like sellers and vice versa. Every part of this book is important to both buyers and sellers. Understanding the goals of the other parties to the transaction will increase your chances of completing an efficient and effective transaction.

Remember to look for gold nuggets — ideas you can use to save or make money. Look for ways to help you make better decisions. Take notes. Highlight. Scribble. If you can't find any gold, here's my *30-day Money Back Guarantee*: Return the book (unmarked) to the place it was purchased. If you purchased directly from our website, mail it (unmarked) to Publisher:

streetsmartbooks, LLC

P.O. Box 2

Middletown, DE 19709-0002.

Copy the receipt and send it also. If it's within thirty days from the date of purchase, I'll send you a check for the full amount you paid for the book.

Checklists at the end of each chapter will test your comfort level with that chapter's subject matter. Use the results to understand the areas in which you need help. Start building your team with professionals who are smarter than you in those specific areas.

street~stats

Statistics from the
Small Business Administration's
Office of Advocacy:

Small Businesses...

- represent over 99% of all employers
- employ 52% of all private workers
- employ 61% of the private workers on public assistance
- employ 38% of the private workers in high-tech occupations
- provide virtually all of the net new jobs
- provide 51% of the private sector output
- represent 96% of all exporters of goods
- receive 35% of federal contract dollars
- are home-based 53% of the time
- are franchises 3% of the time

As you proceed with the process of buying, selling, or evaluating a business, you will discover much about yourself. You will explore your values and the values of others. You will be faced with many right or wrong choices — it will, in fact, be a spiritual journey. You will be making decisions about how you treat others during negotiations, what information to reveal, and how much emphasis you place on the goals of others. Take this opportunity to study exactly who you are — and who you wish to be. Since the world of business often overlooks our spiritual impact on others, I challenge you to be the best you can be and make a difference in the business world around you.

A final word: I've owned and operated small businesses as well as bought and sold them. But my real experience has come from watching the mistakes and successes of others as I practiced business brokerage over the past twenty years. It is always easier to learn from others' mistakes. You would be wise to stick to the basics and use common sense and your best judgment.

Good luck, and enjoy the book!

Samuel S. Tuttle, CCIM.

"Better is a little with righteousness than great revenues without right."

1

Small Business
in America

- The American Dream
- The American Reality

Unless you've been involved in the ownership and operation of your own business, chances are that your understanding of the matter has originated from what you've heard and read from others. That's why the American Dream is so attractive to those thinking about owning their own business. People like to talk about or write about their successes. That's why you hear all the success stories and all the triumphs and pleasures that await you in your new business.

street~stats

According to the Small Business Administration:

In 1998, small business employment (firms with fewer than 500 employees) reached an estimated 55.4 million. Services and retail trade industries represent much of this employment with 20.4 million and 11.5 million respectively.

In addition to employer firms, about 34 million individuals whose primary occupation is self-employment are by definition small businesses.

THE AMERICAN DREAM

You can be the boss! You may feel trapped in a job especially when the "boss" doesn't seem to know what's really happening as much as you do. You punch a time clock or at least have someone watching your comings and goings and you have to answer to them. With your own business you can set the rules! You can take off whenever you want — and your employees will be the ones to stand at attention when you enter.

You can be rich! All you get now is a wage or salary but when you own your own business you can keep all the profits.

You don't have to share with anyone. The money will pile up and up, even after you buy a Porsche and a new country estate.

You can proclaim a vacation any time you want! No more once a year, hurry up and get back, limited time off. You can work when you feel like it and stay home when it suits you.

You can decide which tasks you want to do and make others do the rest! No more menial tasks for you — that's what employees are for. After all, it's your company, isn't it?

You can duplicate yourself! With proper training and motivation, you can create others as talented as yourself and manage them. Now there will be more perfect workers and your company will be the best in the business.

You can make a better mousetrap...and the world will beat a path to your door!

You can have fame, fortune, and then retire early enough to enjoy it all!

Well, that's what you've heard, isn't it? People seem to zero in on the positive when it comes to owning their own business and dreaming about the potential for financial freedom. If you've talked with business owners about their experiences, you probably have a truer vision of the experience contemplated. It is more like the scenario presented in the following discussion — The American Reality.

THE AMERICAN REALITY

Small businesses are really the backbone of the American economy. The successful American company is often the foundation for future corporate giants. Many small firms have been bought out by large corporations (making their founders wealthy) or have grown up into American pillars of profitability. America's small businesses — some 24 million strong (based on business tax return data) — employ about 52% of the private work force, contribute 51% of private sector output, create most

street~stats

According to the Bureau of the Census: Characteristics of Business Owners
Survival Rates of All Firms Existing in 1992 by 1996 (excerpts):

	1992	1993	1994	1995	Firms surviving until 1996
All firms	7.3	6.7	5.8	4.7	75.5
Firms without employees	8.3	7.7	6.5	5.1	72.4
Firms with employees	2.7	1.5	2.3	3.0	90.5
By Industry:					
Manufacturing	5.1	4.6	5.3	3.4	81.6
Wholesale Trade	6.9	6.7	5.6	3.0	77.7
Retail Trade	6.9	4.8	5.5	5.0	77.8
Finance, Ins. & Real Estate	3.6	3.9	6.3	3.7	82.6
Services	8.0	7.3	6.2	4.2	74.3
Not Classified	11.4	9.5	6.6	4.8	67.6

Note: The source also found that of the status of the businesses at closure was successful for 57.4% of the firms with employees and 36.4% for firms without employees. Industry figures are heavily influenced by their ratio of firms with and without employees.

of the new jobs, and produce 55% of innovations.

There are many reasons for business failures, but the leading causes are those that should have been addressed before the businesses ever started. Lack of proper management and/or insufficient experience are the chief problems. While the basics of all small businesses are the same, each business is, in fact, different. You should be looking for one that mirrors your interests, talents, experience, and training. You might even consider working in a similar business for a while before starting your own.

Another common cause of failure is insufficient capital or poor capital management. The financing one uses to purchase or acquire a business if often part of the problem. You wouldn't think about going to sea in a boat without enough gas and water for survival (and return trip), but many fledgling businesspeople choke on poor cash flows and have no reserves to weather the storm that accompanies the steep learning curve of a new business. They often rely on rosy cash projections, usually calculated by others, and then learn the truth the hard way. Lack of a good business plan often leads to a poor estimation of cash required and/or cash flow.

How people feel about themselves in their current positions should not be overlooked. Unhappy employees start to think

street~smarts

You need to know about Dr. Tuttle's Labor Replacement Theory. I developed this theory in the sixties as I looked at the struggling small businesses around me. I noticed the owners of the companies are left to survive on the theoretical profits they forecasted — after paying everyone else. Employees first. Then suppliers. What about the rent and utilities? You wouldn't forget taxes, would you? What often happens in small business is that the owner winds up working for minimum wage (or less), and gets to work a hundred hours a week. In other words, the only money he really makes is the value of his free labor in the business. Sometimes, it's worse than that!

about opening their own businesses. Dissatisfied business owners begin to lose excitement and objectivity. The business can deteriorate quickly with a poor attitude.

Then there's the *Boss Is a Jerk Theory*. You should make every attempt to find out why your boss doesn't seem to know what's going on. Many times he is trusting a specific job to you and doesn't really have time to follow up on what you're doing. This is especially true if you're doing the job well. What you don't see is the time the boss spends scheduling, doing cash flow forecasts, reports to management, estimating and securing income, expense control, and lots and lots of paperwork. When you own the business, all that extra responsibility becomes yours; imagine what your employees are going to say about you!

If you have the drive and desire to own your own business, you are probably one of the few who could be considered a good employee. In today's workplaces, employees frequently adopt the attitude that their jobs exist only to supply their own needs. Not many workers understand that their input is more important than what they take out. The success of their efforts on the job make the company go forward...or backward. If they aren't planning for tomorrow for the company, the chances are the company may not have a tomorrow. Many employees do not want either work or responsibility. Supervisors may have been chosen for their consistency of attendance or, worse yet, for their fine production performance. Neither of these traits necessarily makes a good supervisor. Over and over again, I have seen top sales performers promoted into sales managers who have

slowed, stopped, or even ruined the companies that rewarded them.

When you train new employees, your competitor may send you a thank you note! What often happens after you upgrade a responsible employee is that he goes across the street to your competitor. That's because you didn't explain that the compensation would grow with new responsibilities. Now you have to compete against someone you trained! And for the other guy's profit!

erates from the pit of his stomach. After he reviews and analyzes all the available facts and information, he reaches somewhere south of the brain for the decision. If you don't have it there . . . you don't have it.

When buying or selling a business you want to think about the wages of the employees and about your own income in these terms. What can you do to make your employees more productive and reduce turnover? What perks can be cost-conscious yet effective? Perhaps a title (instead of a raise)?

IN SUMMARY

I have learned after many years of operating small businesses and observing countless others why the grass is always greener on the other side of the fence — it's because of all the fertilizer! Before you start or buy a small business, examine your motives for doing so. Structure some simple goals you hope to achieve. Verify and validate those goals among your family members, close friends and professional advisors. Doing things for the wrong reasons can only cause wrong results. Before you join the ranks of America's small business owners, make sure you do so for the right reasons and that you have realistic and achievable goals.

Throughout this book I will repeatedly tell you that the good businessperson op-

How Ready Are You?

CHAPTER 1 COMFORT ZONE CHECKLIST

Circle the comfort level for each issue.	High				Low
I understand the American Dream	5	4	3	2	1
I understand the American Reality	5	4	3	2	1
I know my goals	5	4	3	2	1
My goals are reasonable	5	4	3	2	1
My goals are attainable	5	4	3	2	1
I am happy where I am	5	4	3	2	1
I am fulfilled where I am	5	4	3	2	1
I have solid life experiences to draw on	5	4	3	2	1
I have talents	5	4	3	2	1
I know where the capital will come from	5	4	3	2	1
I've talked it over with my family	5	4	3	2	1
I've discussed it with counselors	5	4	3	2	1
I can live for six months without much income	5	4	3	2	1
I can live for one year without much income	5	4	3	2	1
I'm ready!	5	4	3	2	1
I think I may be ready	5	4	3	2	1

About your answers: There are no right or wrong answers. Study your responses to determine which items you need help with. Have your spouse or potential partner(s) fill in a copy of the checklist also. Discovering which subjects lack high comfort levels will help you choose professionals with the appropriate skills.

"Seek and ye shall find."

2

How to Choose the Type of Business to Buy

- Inventory your Inputs
- Market Gaps
- Amount of Competition
- Professionalism of Competition
- Manufacturing, Service, or Retail
- Inventories
- Special Skills
- Overhead
- Markups Available
- Dollar Volumes
- Dollars Per Sale
- Equipment Costs
- Other Items
- Franchises

It is true that all small businesses require the same basic management talents – planning, organizing, staffing, directing, and controlling – but all small businesses are different. You can increase your chances of success by choosing wisely. Rather than grabbing the closest opportunity, take your time to study the alternatives and try to choose one that fits your goal strategy. Review the following components and concepts of small business and consider how each would fit into your personal goals.

INVENTORY YOUR INPUTS

What is your background? Even if you are dissatisfied with the type of work you are doing, you have collected valuable experience in the field. The areas you have successfully performed in are no longer unknowns to you. Consider this: How would a farmer do in an independent donut shop? People skills are less important when dealing with agriculture than with retail. This is not to say that a farmer could not be successful in a retail business, but he would probably do better with a retail nursery business than with donuts. Agree? Look at all of the things you have done, including hobbies, and see if there isn't some common thread of interest that will make you better at a specific type of business.

Consider your education. Granted, not all education comes from books. Some of the best education is through company training, seminars, home study, and the excitement of learning about hobbies and special interests. Education is the opposite of ignorance. Stay away from a business about which you are ignorant. Many franchise opportunities offer training and I am not belittling the effectiveness of such training, but the people skills and common sense required to operate many businesses are not easily taught. You should look for a business in which you can claim an edge.

I've already mentioned hobbies, but this is an area that most people overlook so I will mention it again. Do you like to do ceramics in your spare time? Are you a hunter or fisherman? A whiz with needlework or crafts? Do you triumph in the kitchen? Enjoy entertaining? Wonderful with kids? All of these special talents may direct you to a sensible business — one that will satisfy the interests you already have.

Consider your direct work experience. If you've made money for others you've increased your chances of making money for yourself. Try to avoid planning your business around the talents of others — even family members. When I was young in the work force I could never figure out why my bosses didn't understand that they couldn't survive without my services. Finally, one of my bosses told me his secret — the "you could get hit by a truck" theory. He knew that if I got hit by a truck on the way to work he would have to operate without me. He would never let me be indispensable.

Your business needs *you*. To the extent that you depend on the skills or talents of others, you may very well have a "hit by a truck" problem.

Make a checklist of the areas in which you have some experience, training, education or significant exposure. Look for that common thread. Concentrate on finding a business that capitalizes on the central theme of your experience.

SURVEY THE MARKET FOR GAPS

When you decide on the general type of business you might want to buy, you can get a little closer by studying the need for that specific type of business in your area. Major market firms use some fairly simple methods to determine the need for products and services in any given area. They first look for *market gaps*.

Don't let the term throw you. A market gap is just what it sounds like. In the market you are researching, you are looking to see if there is some gap (demand or need) for you to fill. If you have a general idea, for example, retailing, you can use the old Yellow Pages trick. Take a telephone book from a large city or suburb far away from you and compare the Yellow Pages with your own telephone book. Find out what's missing. Compare the number of firms for different services or products. You'll be amazed at how much you can learn from this simple trick.

It's possible to get very specific with the study of market gaps. Most states have a planning office that compiles many statistics. If you live in a state that has a sales tax, the sales tax department also compiles many statistics on expenditures by product as well as by area. Armed with these statistics you can calculate with close precision where the gaps exist. Be sure to use common sense.

street~smarts

I remember one college professor who spent the first thirty minutes of our initial Statistics class writing names, dates, numbers, and formulas on every blackboard in the room. Then he went to his desk at the front of the room, sat down and said, "These are the statistics...what do you want me to prove?"

You can also calculate *slippage*. This is a term for expenditures that should be spent in your area but for one reason or another the money is being spent in some other geographical area. This doesn't have to be a difficult calculation. You might simply survey cities or towns close to you and count the number of firms in each locality. Relate the number of firms to the population of the localities. If you have two pizza shops per 100,000 people and the other locality has four pizza shops per 100,000 people, you have probably found a gap. (Caution: make sure the firms you are counting are making a profit!) Another simple method is to compare the number of square feet of specific business space in two localities. For example, you may find six thousand square feet of women's retail clothing in one area, compared to two thousand square feet of women's retail clothing in another. Again, compare the square footage per population for each area.

STUDY THE AMOUNT OF COMPETITION

Determine how many companies you will have to compete with. This is extremely important. Remember, when you cut the pie into more than eight pieces, there is hardly enough for anyone. You should also scour the community to determine if there are others trying to fill the same gap you are. If you choose a product or service that is otherwise unavailable in your market, find out why it is not available. There is no joy in becoming the first to make a big mistake, nor is there in making the same mistakes as your predecessors — and I've seen that too.

PROFESSIONALISM OF COMPETITION

After you determine the amount of competition, study each operation to see how it is run. Are the staff friendly, courteous, and knowledgeable? Will your staff be? Can you do better? How?

Be on the watch for business closings in your area. Try your best to determine why the business closed. Sometimes there are reasons other than lack of demand. Death of a business owner might cause a busi-

ness to be closed while the demand for products and/or services might actually be on the rise. Businesses can also be zoned out. Under local zoning laws, a change of ownership may cause the loss of special zoning that was required for the operation. Owners might be retiring and feel the business is not worth enough to seek a purchaser. By the way, you don't have to wait until the business closes to know about it. If you're looking for a food business, ask the bread delivery man to keep an eye out for you. He often knows months in advance of a business that needs a new owner.

Look for recent employment shifts or changes. Keep in contact with members of the local Chamber of Commerce. Solicit information from insurance agents, sales people, and the like. Make sure they know the specific area of business you are interested in. If you share your confidence with real estate agents, discuss compensation in advance. And, don't give *any*body more information than you want *every*body to know.

Read the papers every day. Look for fairly recent technology changes. Watch for new products in other areas. Consider national trends as well as local ones. Be careful not to try to force a "California" idea on a "New England" society. As you study the market, try to anticipate trends in your area of interest, whether these involve people, products, or services.

MANUFACTURING, SERVICE, OR RETAIL

Most small business fall into one of these three categories. It's important to understand the primary differences among them. If you have not yet chosen one of these categories, get a pencil and paper and take notes. Record your initial reactions to each item. Does the item excite you? Scare you? Bore you? Your own observations may help direct you to the area you should be pursuing.

Inventories

Required by manufacturing and retail businesses and by some types of service businesses, inventories are costly to purchase and maintain. They require insurance and space for storage. There is always a problem of obsolescence. If it hasn't sold in a while it may never sell. Inventories are subject to pilferage and/or theft. They can be damaged by water, fire, smoke, or a number of other causes. Depending on the diversity of the inventory, you may need a substantial number of suppliers to maintain the items for the business. This raises the question of minimum orders, freight costs, and so forth. If your proposed business is inventory heavy, you will require lots of money to maintain the proper inventory to allow your business to run well.

Special Skills

Either you have special skills or you don't. While you may feel comfortable about hiring someone with the required special skills, the question is will you feel comfortable with replacing the employee if she leaves. Can the business afford the proper compensation to guarantee the continuance of employees with the special skills required? Will future employees with special skills be readily available or will your business suffer interruption?

Overhead

Each business has a unique layer of overhead. Retail space is the most expensive space to lease or buy. A service business that does not require customers to come to your place of business may very well choose a less expensive location. Of course, if you feel you need visibility to compete, you may wind up spending the same as retail. While manufacturing space is generally lower cost (per square foot) you may need substantially more square footage to produce. In addition to the space needed you must calculate secretarial services, bookkeeping services, communications, and other fixed costs. Although advertising is a variable cost, most businesses have a fixed-cost component for Yellow Pages, and so forth. The amount of overhead varies for each type of business and then by each specific business.

MARKUPS AVAILABLE

In many areas, product and brand competition may be very keen, and you may not be able to price your products or services as high as you desire. The amount of profit may be controlled by an oversupply of vendors. Don't get caught playing in that game. If you can't offer a different product or price strategy, you will be infected with the same disease you inflict upon your competition. Consider what Wal-Mart is doing to many small competing businesses.

One of the most important lessons I ever learned about business is this: "You have to make a profit to survive." I know it sounds silly, but many firms think they can make it on volume alone. Remember, negative one multiplied one thousand times is still an overdraft!

DOLLAR VOLUMES

Is there room for error? True, volume is not enough alone, but it is very important. You need enough sales volume (guaranteed) to ensure that overhead expenses become a controllable percentage of sales. In fact, this is the very reason we are taught percentages. Your overhead and other expenses must be controlled to the point where they do not jeopardize the net profit of the operation. More dollar volume is usually like oxygen at 25,000 feet elevation. You can't survive without it.

DOLLARS PER SALE

The higher the price, the fewer sales you need. Sound simple? Not so. The higher the price, the more sophisticated the consumer, the more quality is demanded, the higher the cost of inventory will be, and, probably, the higher your advertising costs will be. There is a correlation between price of product and number of sales needed for a business to operate, but there is no genuine advantage to either higher or lower price items. There is a genuine difference, of that you can be sure.

EQUIPMENT COSTS

Some types of businesses require very expensive equipment. Although it can sometimes be leased and therefore the initial capital requirements may be reduced, the equipment costs do not go away. Then there is the maintenance. If you are smart, you will look at equipment over the long run and add all the costs together. How long will the equipment last? Is it new now? How much maintenance will it require? Will that change with the volume of sales? What will you do when it needs to be replaced? Can it be obtained or replaced without a great loss of business time? Is it readily available? Governmental regulations increase every day. Will new requirements drive your costs up?

OTHER ITEMS

Check to see what's available in your area. But, be cautious. If you are the kind of person considered impulsive or compulsive, surround yourself with conservative advisors. Remember the Bible passage that states, "In the counsel of many is wisdom." To reinforce your staying power in a new business there is no better plan component than forward planning. True, it takes time to plan, but there is no substitute for good planning. Even though you can't see into the future you can base your plans on a series of "what ifs." What if sales do not grow? What if they do? What if competition you didn't expect opens up? What if one closes?

If you have family members who will be involved in your business, or a partner, you would be wise to consider how they might react to different situations. Discuss the "rules" and possible impact of breaking those rules. Who is going to work how much and how often? Who will have how much authority? How much is each going to expect to be paid? Who is contributing money? What if money runs short? Consider the potential stress of the "what ifs." Make sure all those you are counting on can handle the coming stress.

Finally, be realistic about the finances. It is possible to lose everything you invest — and more. If you plan to use borrowed funds, you can depend on the lender's requirements to include your personal guarantee for any borrowings. You could lose everything you have saved and earned over the years. How would you handle that?

When you have developed a basic plan, see if there is a way to leave a back door. This would be some way to get out of the business if things don't go favorably. This is not always possible, but remember the great percentage of new business failures. You may become one of them. One often-used method is to purchase the real property from which the business operates. If the business does not perform to your expectations, you may find a buyer for the business through a favorable lease of the real property. Or you may sell the real property at a profit and recover some of your losses. There is an extra area of risk here, so get good counsel for this part of your plan.

FRANCHISES

To find innumerable franchise opportunities purchase a copy of *Inc.* or *Entrepreneur* magazines. Most franchises offer an information package for free. Some require you to submit detailed personal and financial information first. Your state probably has a franchise department or commission that has a filing on every firm selling franchises in your area. They will provide free or low-cost copies to you.

To Franchise Or Not To Franchise?

People like franchises because they work. A new franchisee does not have to solve all the basic problems of setting up the new business by himself. Training is provided. Consultation is often available after purchase. It is true that there are fees, royalties, and other charges but a franchise should bring you more business than you could draw by yourself. People have been trained for decades by the McDonald's example. At any place from coast to coast you may buy the same hamburger and the same french fries in the same basic atmosphere. Why guess about quality or service when you can know for sure? Here are some tips about evaluating whether or not you want to franchise:

- See what they offer. Ask for a franchise brochure. These are usually free and contain lots of propaganda. They usually will not have all the information you are looking for but they will be a good start. If you want all the information, you may have to make an informal application or even provide financial data about yourself.

- See what they charge. Examine the franchise offering to see what the fees, royalties, and other charges are. Compare one franchise opportunity to the others.

- Check filing statements. Most states require companies that offer franchises in that state to file a complete document. They make it available to anyone who asks. Ask.

- Check with existing franchisees. Before you make your selection you should ask a few franchisees what the weaknesses and strengths of the franchise are. Are they financially strong? Have they honored their franchise agreement? Does the franchise name bring extra customers through the door? Would that business owner choose to franchise if they could start over?

When looking at franchises, compare what they offer. Some offer training, help in setting up the new franchise, regional supervision, name recognition, exclusive territorial rights, and other features. Some of these items are included in the initial franchise fee; others are not.

Unfortunately, many franchises are now keeping the best markets and locations as Company Stores. A necessary task in considering franchises is to talk with existing franchisees and see how they are being treated. If you interview one far enough away from the market you plan to enter, the franchisee will most likely be glad to talk with you. They want the franchise to grow, too.

Ready to Choose your Business?

CHAPTER 2 COMFORT ZONE CHECKLIST

If this book is a library copy, please do not write in it. Photocopy this page instead.

Circle the comfort level for each issue.	High				Low
I have inventoried my background	5	4	3	2	1
I have inventoried my education	5	4	3	2	1
I have inventoried my hobbies/interests	5	4	3	2	1
I have inventoried my direct work experience	5	4	3	2	1
I have inventoried my training	5	4	3	2	1
I have inventoried my business exposure	5	4	3	2	1
I understand market gaps	5	4	3	2	1
I am aware of my market	5	4	3	2	1
I am aware of market changes	5	4	3	2	1
I am comfortable with manufacturing	5	4	3	2	1
I am comfortable with a service business	5	4	3	2	1
I am comfortable with a retail business	5	4	3	2	1
I am comfortable with inventories	5	4	3	2	1
I am comfortable with special skills needs	5	4	3	2	1
I am comfortable with overhead expenses	5	4	3	2	1
I have surveyed the competition	5	4	3	2	1
I understand costs and markups	5	4	3	2	1
I understand the importance of sales volume	5	4	3	2	1
I understand dollars per sale	5	4	3	2	1
I am comfortable with equipment costs	5	4	3	2	1
I am realistic about my finances	5	4	3	2	1
I have developed a basic business plan	5	4	3	2	1
I have considered franchising/franchises	5	4	3	2	1

"Hear counsel, and receive instruction
that thou mayest be wise in thy latter end."

3

Ways to Achieve Goals without Buying or Selling

- Joint Venture
- Incentive-Motivated
    Employee/Manager
- Buy or Sell among Partners or
    Family Members
- Liquidation — Instead of Sale
- Selling to a Competitor
- Sell the Real Property, and ??
- Investment Alternatives
- Compromise with Creditors
- Reevaluate Existing Business
- Rethink your Ideas
- Change Professions
- More Education in your Field

There may be some way for you to achieve your stated goals without buying or selling a business on the open market. Goals are the main theme here. Your main goal may be to invest your money. It may be to get out of a given situation, such as needing a job. Your goal may be to get into a desired situation. Consider some of the possibilities in this chapter to see if there isn't some more preferable way to accomplish your goals without actually buying or selling a business.

JOINT VENTURE

Divide talents, capital, and time between yourself and others and define a way to achieve your goals. You may put up the needed capital for someone better equipped to run a business. You could receive an investment return similar to leaving the money in a bank and participate in the profits of the business. If it's your business now, you might seek to create a joint venture with someone with capital instead of selling. If capital is the only problem, you have a good chance of finding someone to discuss this with. Be sure to be honest in sharing your expectations and formulate the same kind of "rules" you would if you were operating the business with you in control. The key to a successful joint venture is value; each party to the venture must offer a unique value. Because of the value of each partner, the others will want him or her to remain as part of the venture. Remember that value is a perception and each party's perception is bound to be different.

INCENTIVE-MOTIVATED
EMPLOYEE/MANAGER

Become one or hire one. You might run someone else's business for a wage, plus a share of the profits. No purchase would be necessary, and there are many advantages to a business already in operation. You can negotiate the details of a purchase option in advance. You can buy the business at a set price or a price determined by a preset formula, after demonstrating the capability of running the business well. The same holds true for a seller of an existing business. Often, a key employee makes an excellent manager. That person wouldn't be a buyer because he lacks the capital. But they could be your escape from the business. Of course, you are still an advisor to the business, and that will enhance the business's ability to survive and be profitable.

BUY OR SELL AMONG PARTNERS
OR FAMILY MEMBERS

Sometimes a business is placed on the market prematurely. If you have someone in or near the business who might be a purchaser, consider discussing all the options with them first. Why generate the need for sales commissions, advertising, and so forth, if you have the buyer or seller at hand? Sometimes it is easier to get financing for an existing business than for a new one. It may be possible to share loan proceeds with a party who wishes to exit the business. In other words, the business can buy out a partner, using its own borrowing power.

LIQUIDATION — INSTEAD OF SALE

This method generally leaves no loose ends and sometimes is the only real way to get cash out of a business. If the quick sale of all inventory and fixtures will generate enough money for the owners of the business, the complicated process of selling the business may be avoided. In present times, buyers expect assurance that the future cash flow is, in fact, valid. It is not unusual for a buyer to pay a seller over time, using at least part of the business's future cash flow to make the payments. This gives rise to the question, "What if the new owner ruins the business — and its cash flow?" If you decide to liquidate, you need to research the various methods of liquidation, as well as who the potential purchasers of assets and inventory might be. It might even be a competitor. If the inventory is currently marketable, the supplier might repurchase it from you, giving you cash or reducing your debt to him. Many have liquidated inventories through a "Going Out of Business Sale."

SELL TO A COMPETITOR
WHO WISHES TO EXPAND

By selling to a competitor, you are avoiding the open market and saving sales and advertising costs. Be careful about going to a competitor who may tell the world that you are going out of business. Your employees might leave overnight and customers may stop dealing with you because of the rumor. But, all in all, the idea has merit. If you wanted to expand, wouldn't you seek to acquire one of your competitors? You can be sure of this axiom, "A new owner *always* thinks he can improve the quality (and profitability) of an existing business." Use this axiom to your benefit!

It might pay to use a third party to determine which competitors might be interested in growing through acquisition. The third party need not reveal the identification of your business.

SELL THE REAL PROPERTY, AND??

Some of the best business exits I have seen involved no sale of the business itself. The owners held title to the real property, which had significant equity. After selling the real property to access the equity on a permanent basis, they were free to lease the business (with less risk) or to form some type of joint venture for the operation. The business might even lease back the premises from the new owner. They were still in control of the business, in one fashion or another, and had an additional income stream. With the real property equity in cash, they were able to finance the inventory and, in some cases, even the operating capital. This makes a business extremely easy to market, and achieves the maximum sales price.

OTHER TYPES OF INVESTMENT AS ALTERNATIVES

If increased income is really what you want and you have adequate or excess capital, you may not need to buy or sell a business at all. Explore other kinds of investments. Private financing for local auto dealers offers above-average investment returns. Of course, the risk is higher. You should memorize this formula:

Increased Returns = Increased Risk

There's no way around it. If there were exaggerated returns without increased risk, everyone would do it. Then the demand would be increased, reducing the returns.

COMPROMISE WITH CREDITORS

If the only reason you are considering selling your business is because of cash flow problems, call each of your creditors and discuss the problem with management (not the accounts receivable department). Honesty is the best policy and suppliers and creditors would rather work things out with you than lose it all. Be creative in approaching solutions with them and listen to what they have to say. This won't be the first time they have been approached with this problem. If your cash flow is poor, the likelihood of a reasonable sale is greatly reduced. In evaluating small businesses, appraisers abandon all time-honored techniques when they smell distress. If you can't cure the problems, your business may not be saleable at all.

REEVALUATE EXISTING BUSINESS, AND CORRECT

If you are planning to sell your business, the wisest thing you can do is solve all the problems the business has. Who do you think wants to buy a business that has problems? Take a few days off and put your thinking cap on. Take a management or accounting course or seminar. Hire the services of a professional in the area of your problems and find solutions. When you have corrected the problems that have been plaguing you, do not be surprised if you no longer desire to sell. This advice has thwarted many a commission for me but made me some very valuable friends.

RETHINK YOUR IDEAS

You're never too old to learn, especially about yourself. If it's independence you desire, determine what that really means to you. I once had a waterman tell me what being rich meant to him: "Not *having* to work, so you can enjoy your work!" Reexamine your ideas of security, of wealth, and of happiness. Another friend once told me that "true wealth is one cent more than you need." I think I have pretty smart friends.

CHANGE PROFESSIONS

I have often come across businessmen looking to purchase businesses because they were not fulfilled in their present endeavors — IBM executives who would rather operate the proverbial donut shop, and even an airline pilot who wanted to own an auto paint business. Some of them actually completed the purchases but others took my advice to change within their specific talents and experiences. Some became consultants to their former employers (at increased rates). Some changed professions but first admitted they had chosen the wrong profession to start with. A good stepping stone to buying a business is to take a manager or employee position in a similar business. This gives you a realistic look at the business and allows you to see whether you'll really like it or not.

GET MORE EDUCATION IN YOUR FIELD

If you're just not happy with what you're doing, maybe you need a promotion in the

street~smarts

Multi-Level Paradise
Avon. Amway. Good products and good opportunities. You might consider a multi-level business opportunity if you want to have a low entrance cost into business. If you want to start part-time and keep your job, multi-level could work for you. You will have to be good with people to be a success. You should be a good trainer. A good judge of honesty and dependability. A good listener. A good motivator. While the products and/or services may be great, the real money is in building a sales team and receiving a piece of everyone's action.

same field. Prepare yourself and go for it. In the job market, there are leaders and there are followers. Perhaps a change of roles is really what you need.

Before you leap, do all you can to make sure you are doing the right thing. Buying or selling a business is almost irrevocable in some ways. Think of it as a marriage proposal. Use caution. Exercise mature judgment and seek wise advice. Consider all the alternatives before deciding what to do.

Are You Comfortable with these Alternatives?

CHAPTER 3 COMFORT ZONE CHECKLIST

If this book is a library copy, please do not write in it. Photocopy this page instead.

Circle the comfort level for each issue.	High			Low	
Joint ventures	5	4	3	2	1
Incentive-motivated employee/manager	5	4	3	2	1
Transact with partners or family members	5	4	3	2	1
Liquidation	5	4	3	2	1
Sale to a competitor	5	4	3	2	1
Sell the real property (and lease-back?)	5	4	3	2	1
Put my money in alternate investments	5	4	3	2	1
Compromise with my creditors	5	4	3	2	1
Reevaluate my position and correct	5	4	3	2	1
Rethink my ideas	5	4	3	2	1
Change professions	5	4	3	2	1
Get more education	5	4	3	2	1
Get wise counsel	5	4	3	2	1

About your answers: There are no right or wrong answers. Study your responses to determine which items you need help with. Have your spouse or potential partner(s) fill in a copy of the checklist also. Discovering which subjects lack high comfort levels will help you choose professionals with the appropriate skills.

"Seest thou a man diligent in his business? He shall stand before kings."

4

Why Buy an Ongoing Business

- Original Setup
- Proof of Need for
  Service/Product
- Calculated Risk
- Established Leasehold
  Improvements
- Suppliers in Place
- Customer Base and Lists
- Cash Flow
- Yellow Pages and Other
  Advertising
- Phone Number(s)
- Pricing Established
- Trained Employees
- Services in Place
- Used Equipment in Working
  Order
- Eliminate the Seller as
  Competition
- Better Financing May Be
  Possible
- Business Systems in Place
- Better Tax Treatment Possible
- Early Analysis Possible
- To Expand your Existing
  Business

Buying an ongoing business provides what I call the *Platform Concept.* It's one of the main reasons that franchising is so sought after. The number of real entrepreneurs among America's businesses is really quite small. If individuals each had to start up their own business, even more would fail! As you read the following paragraphs, ask yourself if you have the ability (or desire) to generate each of the steps from zero. Many of these areas are in place when you buy a business, even if they are not running properly. And you probably have no idea how long it would take to learn zoning laws, li-

street~smarts

Potential sellers...listen to this!
Discover why buyers may wish
to buy from you in this chapter.

censing, permits, utilities, floor layouts, inventory establishment and controls, and so forth. When you buy someone else's business you are really buying a platform and building your own business from that foundation up.

ORIGINAL SETUP

You've decided to sell a product. What do you do now? Where do you buy the product? How much should you pay? How should it be priced? Do you need a license or permit to engage in sales? What about sales taxes? Do you collect them? What form of business should you use? Sole proprietor, S-Corporation, partnership, or LLC? How large a facility do you need? What about racks, shelves, and the like? What sort of communications will you need? What kind of advertising works? How often? How much? How many employees should you hire? How do you train them? How much should you pay them? This list could go on forever and it seems to do so. Most people buy an existing business because they rec-

ognize that they do not wish to spend the energy, time, or money to reinvent the wheel. The person who can go in from zero and do all of this is the one I call the entrepreneur. Be sure you are ready for it before you begin. At least part of the purchase price can be allocated to *not* having to spend the time, energy, and money to get the business up and running.

PROOF OF NEED FOR SERVICE/PRODUCT

While the need is not guaranteed by the existence of a business, there is less guesswork. Without sales history, there is a danger in determining that a product or service is needed in a given area. Of course you need to be cautious in believing a seller's representations, but at least you have some track record to look at. Better than that, you can check with each supplier to verify the amount of purchases made by the business. When all else fails, do what one of my clients did when considering the purchase of a business in California: He took a part-time job in the business until he felt comfortable he understood the actual sales volume.

CALCULATED RISK

The risk might be higher, or lower, by following in someone else's tracks. But at least there is some sales and financial track records to use to calculate risk. Risk is difficult to assess. The better your understanding of the matter, the more success you will have at minimizing your risk.

ESTABLISHING LEASEHOLD IMPROVEMENTS

Remember the racks and shelves? They are in place when you buy an existing business. They may or may not be adequate for what you want to do. However, it is easier to make changes than to start from scratch. Often the seller will tell you exactly where to go to purchase or lease additional fixtures. He or she even knows how much you should spend. There are often walls, public rest room facilities, signage, carpeting, or vinyl flooring that you would have to purchase if you were going to set up a new business. Sellers don't often remember all the money they spent doing these things. (Let's hope they don't read this book if you're the buyer!)

SUPPLIERS IN PLACE

They may not be the perfect mix of suppliers but you'll be glad you have a list of them. You may add, subtract, or make any changes to the supplier list later, after you have a better idea of what you want from

them. Don't overlook the fact that they may treat you differently than the existing business owner. Ask about quantity discounts, cash discounts, and help in promotions. You can improve your suppliers without changing the list.

CUSTOMER BASE AND LISTS

It is not unusual for businesses to keep track of their customers, including names, addresses, and even phone numbers. This customer base is very valuable. Even if you change the product line you can contact them and tell them about the changes. I know one purchaser who wrote to each and every customer recorded over a five-year period and asked them what additional products he should sell. He *doubled* the sales in less than one year by listening to the established customer base. Zip codes from a customer list are the easiest way to determine where your customers are coming from.

CASH FLOW

Even a poor cash flow is better than no cash flow at all. There are some exceptions, but generally you are better off purchasing a business that has even a minimum level of sales established. The rents and overhead start from day one. If you need to develop sales from zero, you still have to pay all of those costs. Even if the present sales are not sufficient to pay all of the operating costs, the check you will have to write each week or month will be smaller.

YELLOW PAGES AND OTHER ADVERTISING

Fixed advertising often is only published or purchased once a year. When you buy an ongoing business, that advertising is usually in place. There is no way to get it in place with a new business until that time of the year

comes around. Besides, you can monitor how the seller has been spending his advertising money before you make any changes. You will have an opportunity to evaluate the results of that advertising as well. Every little bit of information helps when it comes to establishing an advertising mix.

PHONE NUMBER(S)

Make sure phone numbers are included in the price. There may be nothing worse than trying to get a new phone to ring! This can be a tremendous benefit of buying an ongoing business. Get permission from the seller to keep the phone numbers. The phone company will not release the number to you without written permission; even if the former phone customer has authorized the termination of service. They will only give you the number after it has been terminated and you furnish them with a copy of the written permission from the former phone number owner.

PRICING ESTABLISHED

Established pricing is helpful even if it's wrong. A smart business purchaser will not make many changes until she has studied sales and customer opinion for a month or two. Finding the right pricing is a difficult task. Since pricing affects sales, it takes a lot of tinkering and tediously recorded observations to get to the maximum sales *and* profitability.

TRAINED EMPLOYEES

Current employees are a great benefit — even if you have to re-train them. Also, listen to the seller's opinion about each employee after you have entered into contract with him. Nothing he says before you commit to buy is worth listening to. Think about it. Most new owners like to have a grand opening of their business. This cannot come until after employees are trained (or you'll chase business away). You will have a head start on this one.

SERVICES IN PLACE

Consider all the services that need to be in place at a new location: gas, electric, phone, water, restrooms, trash removal, pest control, and more. You don't have to worry about sizes of pipes, amperes, building codes, and so forth. You may wish to make changes but do that carefully.

USED EQUIPMENT IN WORKING ORDER

If you had to buy used equipment from a vendor, you would probably be very nervous. But when you buy it as part of a business and you're smart enough to buy it "in good working order" you will buy that equipment at the best possible price. Some of it may be better than new equipment, as standards seem to have gone downhill for the past few decades. I have seen purchasers get an actual return of *all* their purchase price (over what they would have had to pay to purchase similar equipment). Sometimes, sellers use their book value when selling assets. This means they are willing to sell their assets at cost less the depreciation they took on their tax returns. I hope you're smiling!

LOCATION

Even if it's not *the* best location, you may not be able to match it with a new store. If you can secure a better location, it may be possible to buy the business and relocate it, but consider that many people (customers) are creatures of habit. Some things are best left unchanged.

ELIMINATE THE SELLER AS COMPETITION

One of the least perceived values is this one. If you were going to open a business with a similar product or service, you would have given up some of your business to the seller. This can be a real value.

BETTER FINANCING MAY BE POSSIBLE

If you are starting your new business from scratch, there is not much flexibility in financing. Most lenders follow the same guidelines and the interest rates do not vary more than a point or so. Seller financing is not like this. For the most part, you may negotiate anything that works between yourself and the seller. Graduated payments, seasonal payments, deferred payments, participation in future profits in lieu of part of the sales price, and so forth. Try these with a bank!

BUSINESS SYSTEMS IN PLACE

Bookkeeping, accounting, scheduling, security, and the list goes on and on. It can be a delight to improve on someone else's system, but it can be a migraine to set one up. Most people prefer to have them in place.

This list is by no means exhaustive or all-inclusive, but you get the idea. Most of the items on this list are not assigned a value by the seller. On your private notes, they may well be worth calculating. The seller may be totally unreasonable in some other area and you want to let him win, if possible. Without discussion of the allocation of purchase price, I can tell you that even when you agree on a price it will mean one thing in your mind and another thing in his.

BETTER TAX TREATMENT POSSIBLE

It is possible to buy an existing corporation or partnership in its entirety and calculate the allocation of purchase price to gain ultimate tax savings. This could work against you, however, and it is always wise to solicit the advice of good tax counsel as part of the purchasing strategy. Buying corporate stock, for example, could completely change the seller's net taxable gain (as opposed to buying assets of the corporation). It could also affect the amount of depreciation you would be entitled to. Consult your accountant or tax advisor. The price you pay for the assets, according to the contract, will determine the amount of depreciation you may use to offset income from the business. When you buy the stock of a business instead of the assets, the depreciation amounts used by the seller must be used on your tax returns. The IRS does not like it when you purchase goodwill. They call it "excess over basis." You would be better off, for tax purposes, to amortize the cost of a *covenant not to compete* over the life of that agreement instead.

EARLY ANALYSIS POSSIBLE

Buying an existing business may give you a fairly complete business and market analysis before you open for business. This is speculative, at best, when there is no existing business. This early analysis must not place undue confidence in numbers supplied by the seller, as the results might easily be misleading. All in all, however, a wise purchase of an existing business should reduce risk.

TO EXPAND YOUR EXISTING BUSINESS

The purchase of an existing business, complete with existing customers, can be a wise way to expand your present business. Even if the two businesses are operated differently, you could change one or both to accommodate the best of both worlds.

Do These Things Have Real Value?

CHAPTER 4 COMFORT ZONE CHECKLIST

If this book is a library copy, please do not write in it. Photocopy this page instead.

Circle the comfort level for each issue.	High				Low
Value of platform concept	5	4	3	2	1
Proof of need for services or products	5	4	3	2	1
Calculating risk	5	4	3	2	1
Leasehold improvements	5	4	3	2	1
Suppliers in place	5	4	3	2	1
Customer base & lists	5	4	3	2	1
Existing cash flow	5	4	3	2	1
Ongoing advertising	5	4	3	2	1
Current pricing	5	4	3	2	1
Trained employees	5	4	3	2	1
Getting services/utilities established	5	4	3	2	1
Purchasing equipment & fixtures	5	4	3	2	1
Choosing a location	5	4	3	2	1
Getting new financing	5	4	3	2	1
Business systems in place	5	4	3	2	1
Understanding tax treatment for businesses	5	4	3	2	1
Early market analysis	5	4	3	2	1

About your answers: There are no right or wrong answers. Study your responses to determine which items you need help with. Have your spouse or potential partner(s) fill in a copy of the checklist also. Discovering which subjects lack high comfort levels will help you choose professionals with the appropriate skills.

"A faithful man shall abound with blessings:
but he that maketh haste to be rich shall not be innocent."

5

Why Sell an Ongoing Business

- Change of Lifestyle
- Retirement
- Move Up, or Expand
- Distress
- Family Difficulties
- Move Geographically
- Change of Financial Goals
- Burnout/Brown Out
- By Plan
- Partnership Problems
- The Big Score

The decision to sell your business is never an easy one. While we discuss the process of selling your business in chapter 7, you must first decide this is what you want to do. How does one make that decision? It is largely done based on the personal situations of the owners. You don't sell because a business is performing poorly. You don't sell because a business is performing well. You sell because your goals or personal situation have changed.

tire already but need the freedom from the business to get your start. Buyers: Although many sellers tell buyers this is their motivation, it is not always true. Ask questions about how the seller plans to enjoy retirement. Find out his source of income for the retirement. Is it all going to come from you? Has the business really yielded the kind of income one needs to retire? If not, will it do so for you?

CHANGE OF LIFESTYLE

Let's face it — everyone gets bored after a while. Even the most successful owners may start looking at other ventures. He may need to sell the business to be able to make the change. There are as many variations of this theme as there are people. As a buyer, try to quantify this desire, if possible. Every clue to the seller's motivation is valuable to you. It not only tells you about the business person, it tells you about the business.

MOVE UP, OR EXPAND

A small business person may feel stifled in a small business and desire to move up to something more challenging. There's nothing wrong with this motivation but be certain you have acquired the skills you need before you try to expand. The larger business is not more easily run; it will require more from you — more skills, perhaps more time, and, most certainly, more money.

RETIREMENT

Don't presume the attraction to retirement happens at any particular age. The mood to retire happens as early as thirty-five for some people and as late as seventy-five to eighty for others. You may be able to achieve your retirement goals by selling your business. Or you may have enough assets to re-

DISTRESS

Although the following areas of distress may easily prompt a business owner to sell, most buyers will get cold feet if they sense that distress is the primary motivation. They fear they will wind up with the same distress. Distress comes in many different forms but there are some common areas that require relief.

Personal

Stress is a common cause. The business may demand too much from you. It may actually be too easy or the business to slow. It could throw you into stressful boredom. Imagine the liquor store owner who begins going to church and feels he can no longer sell alcohol.

Reasons for stress in business are not unlike stress in other areas of your life. Marriage, birth, death, and any major life change may produce the personal distress that causes one to decide to sell a business. Some businesses are reputedly easy to run. Let's take just one example — the food service business.

Honestly speaking, the foodservice business is for the young. Restaurant startups require many, many hours per week and even long-established operations need good management starting long before the doors open and ending long after they are locked at night. Like many other businesses, there are unseen areas of the food business. When do you change the menus? How often? Should you change pricing, menu items, suppliers? Are you attracting the right kind of patrons for maximum profitability? And more. These are areas of importance that most people do not consider when they see the food being prepared and served and the cash register ringing. They don't stop to wonder how the place is kept clean, sani-tized, and insect- and rodent-free. They don't consider who maintains the equipment, how often it is replaced, and what is done when it breaks down (usually in the middle of the lunch rush!).

The pressures of the myriad business decisions and the demand of making them on time is only made worse when there is more than one owner involved. More likely than not, multiple owners disagree even on minor issues. While all of these are problems that can be contained or largely eliminated, they all lead to personal stress. Not everyone can handle stress.

Market

Just when you seem to have a handle on the market, it is likely to change. The introduction of new technology, new trends, new products, and new advertising techniques can change your market overnight. Undercapitalized businesses cannot react quickly enough to avoid the distress market changes can introduce to a small business. By the time you realize you have to change to meet market demands, it may be too late.

Obviously, a new competitor will change the market, as will the withdrawal of one. There is always a positive side to change but you need to constantly be in position to take advantage of the changes. Otherwise these changes will impose stress on you *and* your business.

Financial

If you are not fortunate, you may find yourself in the wrong place, or at the wrong time, or with the wrong people. Although this does not initially sound like the foundation for financial distress, the cost of mismanagement is usually very high. Again, the undercapitalized business is a high risk when it comes to the need for additional finances. But we have never defined how much capital is enough for a business. That's because we don't have a crystal ball. We will discuss some rules of thumb in chapter 6, but the rules will not cover every situation. Every business is different.

Employees

Good employees are hard to find — and easy to lose. A good business owner will plan to use negative and positive means to develop and guide his employees — to keep them happy as well as productive. But that sounds easier than it actually is. Too much positive and they will feel like they deserve a better position. If you don't give them one, they will leave. Too much negative and they will leave quickly. No business escapes the threat of distress caused by employee shortages or turnovers.

FAMILY DIFFICULTIES

Business owners often wish to sell because obligations impose hardships on their families. The reverse of this is also true. Sometimes the families impose the difficulties on the business. They consume goods and/or services without paying. They agree to be employees, then set their own schedules. They require finances from the business (or business owner) that are simply not available. If you are one of those status seekers who wants everyone to think you're rich because you own your own business, you are setting yourself up to be taken advantage of. These difficulties may drive you right out of your business. If divorce is an issue, the business sometimes must be sold to provide the funds for a settlement agreement.

MOVE GEOGRAPHICALLY

When business owners want to move to another geographical area, they usually cannot take the business with them. Although this is a good reason to sell, buyers may first want to understand why you are willing to leave a perfectly good business to move. Why not stay around to collect the profits from your business? As a seller, you better have good reasons and be able to communicate them to a prospective buyer. If you can't, the value of the business will be seriously affected.

CHANGE OF FINANCIAL GOALS

Your financial goals can become more ag-gressive or less aggressive. A new stage in life often results in changed goals. If you are tied into a business that regulates you more than you wish, you may decide the only way to achieve your goals is to sell the business.

BURNOUT/BROWN OUT

Burnout is not unusual. In the course of their business or professional careers, many find themselves without the proper motivation to continue. If you're smart (and lucky?), you may spot the signs early enough to do something about it. If not, it only gets worse. Many businesses for sale feature burned out owners. Under these circumstances, a buyer should determine what areas of the business have been neglected and what the cost will be to remedy the situation. This reason for selling will substantially reduce a selling price. If you see it coming, take the time to spruce up your business before you put it on the market. Selling a freshly washed and waxed car is much easier than selling one that needs a cleaning.

BY PLAN

The true entrepreneur is the one who starts or buys a business, manages it to near its maximum potential, then sells the business. Very few people are capable of making a living by doing this. Since we have already stated that every business is different, this entrepreneur takes a risk every time he or she buys or starts a new business. The true entrepreneur actually thrives on the challenge. The price for such a business will be a bit high, but you would be wise to pay the price. What he or she has created will be a money machine for you, if you don't try to fix it.

PARTNERSHIP PROBLEMS

People change. Their expectations of each other are never quite the same. The only resolution when partners get angry or disappointed or tired with each other may be to sell the business. If you encounter this situation, be aware that each partner will have his own goals in the sale of the business. One may need cash. Another may prefer income over time. A third may do anything you can think of just to get out of the difficult situation.

THE BIG SCORE

Buyers want to avoid sellers looking to make the big score. Everyone knows you can sell your business and retire to the Bahamas for life! I have seen quite a few intelligent people fall into the trap of thinking that a business is good just because the price is high. Actually, as you will see when we discuss the valuation of business components, there is really no correlation between value and price in the normal marketplace. Don't let someone make the big score on you.

Which of These Is your Real Motivation?

CHAPTER 5 COMFORT ZONE CHECKLIST

If this book is a library copy, please do not write in it. Photocopy this page instead.

Circle the comfort level for each issue.	High			Low	
I understand my motivation	5	4	3	2	1
I need a change of lifestyle	5	4	3	2	1
I want to retire	5	4	3	2	1
I want to move up or expand	5	4	3	2	1
I am experiencing personal distress	5	4	3	2	1
I am experiencing market distress	5	4	3	2	1
I am experiencing financial distress	5	4	3	2	1
My employee problems are causing stress	5	4	3	2	1
I am experiencing family difficulties	5	4	3	2	1
I am considering relocation	5	4	3	2	1
My financial goals have changed	5	4	3	2	1
I am suffering brown out	5	4	3	2	1
I am suffering burnout	5	4	3	2	1
It has been my plan to sell for some time now	5	4	3	2	1
I am having partnership problems	5	4	3	2	1
I want to make the BIG SCORE	5	4	3	2	1

About your answers: There are no right or wrong answers. Study your responses to determine which items you need help with. Have your spouse or potential partner(s) fill in a copy of the checklist also. Discovering which subjects lack high comfort levels will help you choose professionals with the appropriate skills.

"For which of you, intending to build a tower, sitteth not down first, and counteth the cost, whether he have sufficient to finish it?"

Buying a Business

- Determine your Goals
- Examine the Alternatives
- Hire a Professional
- Check with your Accountant
- Check with your Attorney
- Check All Purchase Information
- Reasons Sellers Withhold Information
- The Hazards of Demanding too Much Information
- Buying a Business Is More than Numbers
- What Assets to Buy
- Valuation of Assets
- Goodwill: Excess over Basis

You would be surprised, no, *amazed* at the way some people go about buying a business. You might think they were buying a pair of trousers or a skirt. They have no more concept of a business plan, adequate provision for finances, or understanding of comparative values in the marketplace than the janitor of the business they are avowed to purchase. Buying a business with the design of having a successful future takes a lot of skill and investigation. Probably the reason you have purchased this book is because you knew it wasn't that easy. But, using some of the techniques in this book is not a guarantee of success either. Good planning and goal setting will prepare you to handle the matter more effectively and alert you to a problem or two.

DETERMINE YOUR GOALS

Do not select the business and then determine your goals. That is putting the cart before the horse. Many buyers before you have failed using this defective reasoning. Things you should be asking yourself are:

- How much time do I want to spend in my new business?
- What personal strengths do I intend to employ?
- How can I use my talents and experience?
- How much income do I need to have from the business?
- How long will it take to get the business to an even pace?
- Where do I want to be in five years?
- How about in ten years?
- How many employees can I probably handle?
- Will I have supervisors and / or managers?
- How much capital do I have to invest?
- Can I afford to lose it all (if the business fails)?
- What will my exit strategy be if

things don't go well?
- Will my family be involved? To what extent can I count on them?
- For how long?

EXAMINE THE ALTERNATIVES

With your goals clearly outlined on paper, search out a complete list of alternative ways to achieve your goals. Scour the community and the marketplace for ideas. Ask business friends for their opinions, and about their particular businesses. Assuming you wish to start or purchase a business (remember chapter 4), begin to decide on the type of business you will be trying to find. If it will be a product sales business, begin to focus on the general type of product(s). If it is a service business, begin to focus on the general type of service(s). Check each alternative against your list of goals and rate each alternative against the other. Prioritize the list of alternatives and continue comparing them with each other.

HIRE A PROFESSIONAL

Like so many things in life, this sounds easier than it actually is. What is a professional? Many states require a license to help people buy or sell a business, usually a real estate license. Those that are licensed have certain qualifications, you may be sure. But what are those qualifications? To know the real estate law will not help you much. Other states have no regulations at all for this area of specialization. There are even companies and franchises that specialize in helping people buy and sell businesses. They do not have any guarantees. Some of them, you will discover, have no more expertise than you do. Some of them will actually have less. Some of them are part-timers trying to make an extra buck. They have special forms (some of which are very good) but no amount of caution is overkill when it comes to selecting a professional in this field. The only way to qualify a professional is to ask for a list of references and check them thoroughly. Choose clients who have been satisfied for a period of years if you want to be sure.

When you choose a professional who helps people buy and sell businesses you enter into the world of agency. If the professional has listings of businesses for sale, she probably represents the sellers. A subagent of the broker that represents the seller still represents the seller. If her first obligation is to the seller, will she be able to help you structure the lowest cost and most effective offer to purchase the business? Not unless she totally lacks ethics. Some say, "There is no such thing as dual agency." It is also said, "You cannot serve two masters." I agree.

If you are fortunate enough to find a

seasoned professional, one whom you have checked out to your satisfaction, ask him to represent you. If he is willing to do so, you can enter into a *Buyer's Broker Representation Agreement.* You can agree to a fee, a fee plus expenses, or a percentage of the purchase price of the business you actually buy. Be careful to use the same common sense and caution you would use with any other professional. Do not advance large sums of money. You only need results-oriented representation. Set limits on the amount of money he can spend. Make sure the agreement is for a specific period of time. Discuss, and then make sure the agreement has language covering the possibility of his company having a listing on a potential purchase. The only way the agent could honestly represent you in that case is if the company was willing to give up the listing and then represent you. Two sales people from the same company should not represent both the buyer and the seller. Since the company usually makes the promises and then stands behind the agents or employees, this is just another case of dual agency.

CHECK WITH YOUR ACCOUNTANT

If your accountant is not the one you plan to use in the business, do not use him to review the purchase details. You should be using the accountant who is going to represent you before the IRS to set up your original books and records. His advice is most crucial at the beginning. He will set up your depreciation and amortization schedules for tax purposes and his advice in structuring the offer will be most valuable. It would be a good idea to check with the accountant back at the "examine alternatives" stage. He may even help you find the other professionals you are looking for. Just make sure they're not brothers. Your accountant should have a book that lists different types of businesses, the average expenditures for each type of expense category, and relative information about revenue possibilities. Here is a good one: *Annual Statement Studies* by Robert Morris Associates, Philadelphia, PA. Available in book form or on disk, it lists businesses by SIC codes. RMA can be reached at 800-677-7621. This type of resource can be used to check the pulse of your intended purchase to see if it is strong or weak.

The accountant is a good source for preparing estimates of profit and loss, capital requirements, and cash flow forecasts. Do not let your accountant dictate to you what to offer for the business. That is your job. Get his advice on matters of accounting, comparative statistics, and basic taxation for the business. It is a good idea to show him your last several years' tax returns and let him comment on how the future business will affect your overall taxation picture.

CHECK WITH YOUR ATTORNEY

Consult with an attorney who specializes in small businesses. Lawyers today choose areas of specialization early in their careers (sometimes before they leave law school). You need an attorney who is familiar with the laws and regulations involving business operations, the types of entities utilized to own and operate businesses, and taxation. Don't forget to check their references. If the attorney has a good working relationship with the accountant, it will help you in the long run. You don't want to get into the position where each one blames the other for some area of overlap.

The attorney should not make your decisions for you. You should consult him about the legal ramifications of the proposed contract and for advice on areas your contract does not cover. Since many small businesses involve the purchase or lease of real property, your attorney should spend a considerable portion of billing time in this area. Ask a lot of questions. Discuss fees in advance and ask for a schedule in writing. You should ask your attorney to review all forms and contracts for "legal sufficiency." The right attorney will envision what could go wrong (legally) and how a court would look at it — according to the document. Many potential pitfalls can be avoided by clear and unambiguous agreements.

CHECK ALL INFORMATION AVAILABLE ABOUT THE PROSPECTIVE PURCHASE

Reasons for selling

Ask candidly why the seller is not going to stay with the business. Be wary if she cannot tell you clearly. Ask a lot of questions, then try your best to verify that what she is saying is, in fact, true. It often happens that buyers inherit all of the seller's problems. You need not refuse to buy a business because it has problems, but problems may affect the purchase price and the amount of capital and talent you need to make the business work. If a broker or agent is involved in the sale, ask him the reasons for selling also. The agent is liable for any misrepresentation or con-

street~smarts

My father always told me, "When someone tells you something, they are either lying or telling the truth." You should try to uncover which is the case.

cealment on his part. While misstatements of facts or opinions made by the seller or the seller's agents do not change the business situation, they may allow you to recover an award for damages and/or bring charges of fraud when things go wrong.

Get past sales figures

Many sellers will tell you that they don't record all sales on the books. Be extremely wary of anyone who makes this remark. Your optimism (or greed) may cause you to want to believe that sales are better than recorded on the books but how could you possibly be sure? The seller may drive a Ferrari and own four houses, but how do you know that the money came from the business you are planning to buy? It really doesn't pay to cheat the government. You will spend the rest of your life looking over your shoulder for the IRS or some other government agency. Discount all such statements when making your decision about any business.

Years ago, I was hired to help a client who wanted to purchase a restaurant/deli in California. Although I always insist on clients making their own decisions, I really didn't like this particular opportunity. There was something wrong. I could feel it in my bones! My client wanted to proceed with an offer, so we did. In the purchase agreement, I asked for access to the purchase records, payroll information, a copy of the lease, and to inspect the checkbook records and stubs, and the monthly bank statements for the past year. The seller agreed to all terms and conditions. In the course of my personal inspection of the books and records, I saw that the seller was taking $1,000 per week as a salary. I later noticed he had deposited the same $1,000 each week, recording it as sales. Knowing his business would be for sale a year in advance, he had overstated both sales and net profit by $52,000 in one year! Of course we did not go forward with the purchase.

Get sales figures for as far back as the seller will go. A minimum should be three years, assuming the business has been in existence that long. Get the sales figures by month. This will allow you to see whether there are certain times of the year that are poor (or strong) in sales. If the business is seasonal and you are buying at the beginning of the poor season, you will need more capital to operate until the peak season arrives. Try to get the sales by department, or product, or service performed. In this way you can see where the bulk of the revenues are coming from. By looking at the relative cost of sales, you may find products or services that can be discontinued and those that might be aggressively marketed to make the business better. Almost every buyer whom I have represented has felt that they could operate the business better than the seller. Buyer's sometimes see a tired seller and, by projecting their enthusiasm and energy, believe they can do better. If this were true, it might pay to open up across the street from the seller and show him how it's done. It may, in fact, be cheaper to do so. The conservative approach to buying a business is to base financial projections on the lowest cash flow that can be substantiated. You probably have plans to make the business more profitable, but this should not affect the price you offer for the business. You should only pay for present value. If you can make the business more profitable in the future, the value will increase.

If you are in a state that has sales taxes, verify all sales information by asking for copies of the sales tax returns. The seller may cry, maintaining that he doesn't report all sales. But, by getting this information you have two things going for you. You will learn minimum sales you can expect to generate and, also, you have caused the seller to make representations (in the form of numbers). Any financial information furnished by the seller can be considered a representation. These documents may later substantiate that your decisions were based on false information.

In some states there is a separate requirement for reporting of gross sales, usually monthly or quarterly. If this is true in your state you should request copies of these filings.

There are ways to verify sales figures. I know of a buyer who asked the bread supplier how many rolls he delivered weekly. After explaining that he might be the new owner of the business and continue to purchase, the supplier became most helpful. He volunteered the information and then went on to compare this business with the ones across town and in the region. He further related that this business's purchases had steadily increased over the last two years. A wealth of information is available if you stop to think where it might be. First determine the questions you want answered — then who should have the answer. Use common sense and creativity.

If you think the reported sales may be less than actual sales, you may want to make your own calculations. Take the amount of purchases (cost of goods sold) and divide by the gross profit percentage that is usual for the type of business. The result of this calculation should be the actual sales. I think it would be wiser to use reported sales in any situation where you are being led to believe that not all sales are being reported.

One final word on this subject. If you find a seller who lies or misrepresents to you, the best thing you can do is walk away. If you transact with someone who you know is misrepresenting information to you, you are buying the proverbial "pig in a poke." Even a cheap price can be expensive!

Construct profit and soss statements

Once you have established even the minimum sales you can expect and know what the fixed costs are going to be, you have almost no need to use a seller's profit and loss statements. Using industry-standard percentages, you or your accountant can actually construct profit and loss Statements (which may be more accurate than those provided by the seller). In this exercise, you can integrate the changes you intend to make to improve the business. You may plan to add personnel or use less labor. You may plan to increase prices or reduce them. In any case, your projections will include your purchase price financing costs. Although the seller's inventory may be completely debt free you may have to either finance it or invest the capital to pay for it. Although the investment of capital may not strongly affect a profit & loss statement, it will surely change the cash flow forecasts beginning with day one.

Determine rents (or mortgage amounts)

If a lease is involved, get a copy. The rents may be scheduled for increases in the future and you need to know this. The lease may be running out and may not be renewable. The seller may not have a valid lease. If a purchase of real property is part of the sale, it may pay you to view the mortgage payments, together with the taxes and insurance, as equivalent to the cost of lease payments. It is often advisable to purchase real property in your personal name (or through an entity controlled by you personally, such as an LLC) and lease the property to your business. In essence, you will have limited control over your income tax liabilities. Both your accountant and attorney may have advice for you on this matter.

Determine fixed overhead costs

These are the costs that do not vary with the amount of sales in the business. Theoretically, if you have zero sales, you would still have to pay these costs. There are items on the profit and loss statement that have a fixed component as well as a variable component. Take advertising for example. If you purchase Yellow Page advertising, the cost is fixed over the course of the year. You may spend more on advertising or you may not. This gives rise to the variable part of the expense. Running a profitable business is easy; you generate enough sales to make the fixed costs become a lesser percentage. This leaves percentages left over, which we call *profit*. Once you determine what *your* fixed costs will be, you can then project your anticipated sales (at varying levels) and see how much volume *you* need to be profitable.

Get payroll information

Every business must keep good records on employees and related costs. Request Federal forms #940 and #941. Even though you may make changes in the amount of payroll, pay close attention to what the seller has spent. Sometimes he's a lot smarter than you think!

Get all other information available

Ask for everything you can think of. The seller probably will resist, and may even refuse, but that is her prerogative. Sometimes sellers will give you copies of their complete tax returns. Sometimes they give you their balance sheet (I wouldn't). You can learn much about the actual cost of their assets. If the seller has private records, ask for them. Get all the information you can. Again, this information is considered by the courts to be a representation. It helps to let the seller know that the information is being requested by your attorney or accountant. For some strange reason, some sellers will allow their accountant to give information to your accountant, even though they refuse to give it to you. Try it.

REASONS SELLERS WITHHOLD INFORMATION

A prudent seller may not reveal private information until a valid offer has been made and accepted. This is reasonable if he is relying on one of the reasons listed below. It is best to determine if the reason for withholding information is a valid one. Ask for the reason.

Competitors would like the information

What would stop a competitor from "inquiring" about the sale of a competing business and then using the information gained to compete? Nothing. It happens all the time. Although you need the information

outlined on the previous pages to make the best decisions, you don't need this type of information before making an offer. If it is necessary to make a bona fide offer first, don't be afraid to do so. The offer must have specific clauses in it to protect you, however. You should contract to have all of your deposit money returned if you do not buy the business based on your reaction to the information supplied. The price should be firmly fixed; that is to say that it cannot be increased once the seller proves to you that the business is worth purchasing.

Afraid of IRS

I personally know of cases in which employees of government agencies have posed as buyers and solicited private records. In one case, it resulted in jail time and a one million dollar judgment. If the seller is not breaking the law, he should not worry about this, but you will hear it more often than you would believe. If the seller is violating the law, do you want to trust that he will not violate you?

Isn't really sure of the figures herself

Not everyone keeps good records. In small businesses, it is not unusual for the business owner to turn over manila envelopes of cash register tapes to the accountant. Actually, this is not smart. If you don't take responsibility for understanding the figures in your business, you increase your chances of failing. The accountants do not like this form of communication, either. It turns them into bookkeepers, and their bill to you is likely to be much larger than you want to pay. They prefer everything in columns, totaled, when they receive it. Then your accountant can advise you more effectively. However, it is not always done this way and many business owners are really not sure of the figures you are requesting. I know of one successful business owner who uses the "In-Out" method of accounting for profitability. If more comes "In" than goes "Out," the business is doing all right. The business I am speaking of grossed over three million dollars per year the last time I checked. Of course, you can see the problem with this. If you don't pay all bills promptly, or if you don't receive all payments promptly, a cash flow problem could sneak up on you before you know it.

Price and terms must first be agreed upon

Imagine yourself as a seller. After you provide all the requested information, including some very private material, the potential purchaser offers $10,000 instead of $100,000. Or, the purchaser offers full price but offers no money down. You're probably not going to accept the offer and you've spent a lot of time and energy to provide the information for nothing. Not only that, but your personal business information has gone through a dozen hands that never should have seen the figures. It is not a good idea to negotiate price before you see the figures, but you can understand why a seller would like to do so. If you make an offer, and then see that the numbers do not justify the offer, it is not the end of the world. Rescind your offer and make a lower one. Discuss your findings with the seller and ask him to justify the price. Get more information that will support a higher price. I have seen some interesting reactions when a serious buyer has asked a seller to justify his selling price. Some sellers stated a price because their agent suggested it. They were willing to accept much less.

Seller wants to see your financial strength first

This is a smart seller. Why should she give you all of her information until she is sure you have the financial strength? If a seller asks you for your financial statements, do not be offended. You may not wish to supply these until you have seen certain financial information. That is up to you. Do not view her request of your financial statements as a sign that the business is strong or weak. She may simply have been advised to do so. It's up to you whether you supply the information or not. If it can't hurt you and it will cause the seller to supply the requested information, you may wind up competing with fewer possible purchasers. For each person who refuses to give her information, there is one less potential purchaser.

He doesn't trust anyone, either

The seller is a real person, just like you. Take the time to understand why he won't part with the necessary information, and then negotiate. Offer your financial statement (only if it is strong) before he asks you for it. Take him to lunch and ask all the questions you want to. At the close of the meeting, request that he back up the provided information to your accountant. Empathize with him, then demand the information. Reason with him. Do what you need to do, but do not purchase a business without getting the representations you need to consider.

THE HAZARDS OF DEMANDING TOO MUCH INFORMATION

Although you need all the information you can get to make your decision, there are times when demanding too much information can actually backfire on you. A seller has no way of determining your level of interest until you reveal it to him. It is pos-

street~smarts

Offer Attachments
When making an offer it may be a good idea to attach items that will make the seller consider your offer more favorably than others. You might offer your financial statement and a short biography of your business experience or otherwise demonstrate your ability to finance the proposed transaction. If more than one offer is presented, yours will be the one that answers some of the seller's questions. If you are asking for seller financing, this could backfire. The seller would see your assets and/or net worth and would negotiate to get the most he could. In that case you might have given too much information.

sible that he may misinterpret your demand for more information than you need to make an offer. Offers are usually made subject to a buyer's verification of detailed information. After an offer is accepted and price and terms have been negotiated, you will then want to inspect payroll records, bank deposit records, and so forth. If you ask for detailed information before you make a written offer, some of the following reactions may occur.

The price may go up

The seller may feel you are too interested, and either raise the price or refuse to negotiate a lower price.

The seller may be offended

My personal feeling is — let him be offended. I am going to purchase a potentially successful business and want to lower my risk in the selection process. I feel it is good practice to explain this to a seller so that he can understand that my motives are to buy — not look. This has changed many a seller's attitude.

The time delay could cost you the purchase

While you are playing around with the numbers, someone else could slip in and buy the business you're looking at. It has happened. However, that purchaser may be taking a much higher risk than you desire. There is always another business to look at. If you purchase with this attitude, you will be under much less pressure when making your decisions.

The information could be misleading or defective

Some well-meaning sellers will invent information because you require it. They estimate the sales by month or sales by department using their overall knowledge of the business. This is okay if they explain to you what they are doing, but sometimes they forget to tell you.

BUYING A BUSINESS IS MORE THAN NUMBERS

The concentration on numbers, facts, and figures might draw away from the real process at work in buying a business. The seller's numbers may not be your numbers. You may not do as well. His personality might be the reason for much of his revenues. If this is the case, you may see a drop in sales. Correspondingly, your personality may cause an increase in sales. Either way, don't lose sight of the fact that you have decided to purchase a business to achieve the goals you have set for yourself. You might buy a business in spite of the numbers but it can still be an informed decision. When it comes to the numbers, however, you can write an offer "subject to" and "conditioned upon" the verification of figures and events in the business. There is some real protection in knowing the representations of the facts and figures.

WHAT ASSETS TO BUY

This is an area that demands negotiation and a clear understanding of the nature of both

Warning! The highest potential of miscommunication or misleading information is in the representation of numbers, facts, and figures. I'd like to put this on every page of this book!

the assets and the business. The object is to buy only the assets that have real value, and to purchase all the assets you will need to operate the business. The theory is one called *turnkey*. When you complete the purchase, all you want to have to do is "turn the key" in the front door to operate. This, of course, is a bit simplistic. In fact, you may be making subtle changes in the business, maybe even major changes. Remember, of the assets that exist in the present business, you only want to purchase the ones that will be efficient and effective in your new operation.

Only desirable inventory and equipment
The seller is in the best position to return undesirable inventory or sell unwanted equipment. You will be a new account for suppliers and the chance of negotiating the return of merchandise without increasing your future purchase costs is slim. Chances are that the seller has an open account with

suppliers and can return undesirable or excess inventory for a credit. Suppliers view credits to the seller quite differently than they would to a new account. If you do not plan to use some of the present equipment, let the seller exclude it from the sale and let her sell it (or junk it). You won't have time to do this and it's not really your responsibility. If she desires a sale, she'll have to cooperate. If she decides not to cooperate, perhaps you can discount your offer by the amount you feel is justified for the unwanted equipment. You will, won't you?

Only current merchandise and equipment
More specific problems arise from inventory or equipment that is obsolete. You cannot afford to buy merchandise that will never sell or equipment that is no longer functional. It may cost more to repair obsolete equipment than it would to replace it with modern technology. Parts may not be available at all. Anything you pay for these items is extra cost. As part of the inventory and equipment evaluation, it would be wise to hire an independent firm to count and set a value on both. Make it clear to the firm that you do not wish to purchase anything obsolete. They should know what obsolete is and they will explain it to you.

Inventory at verified cost
Use an independent appraiser to deter-

mine the cost. Never use retail price. You are buying the business, not the goods. The seller paid only cost and you cannot pay more. The purchase contract should allow for your approval of all purchases after the date of the contract, so the seller will not stick you with purchases you would not have made. Never include a fixed inventory cost in the purchase price of the business, but allow the value to fluctuate with actual inventory. Otherwise, the seller could sell all the inventory while you are waiting to settle on the business. He could then not restock and charge you the same amount. He would have all the extra cash. One way to limit inventory fluctuations after signing the contract is to set a range of limitation. An example of such a limitation could be "the value of inventory will not be ten percent more or less on day of settlement." Agents like the inventory to be part of the sales price — it increases their commission! Say no!

Furniture and fixtures

Furniture and fixtures are personal property items included in the purchase price. These are items that are movable and not attached to the real estate. Items that are attached, usually by screws or bolts, will either be leasehold improvements or trade fixtures. These items will be discussed in the following sections.

Examining a list of personal property included in the sale is an opportunity to use a magnifying glass to see exactly what you're purchasing. A complete list of the furniture and fixtures needs to be part of the contract. The value of each item is not necessary, but your understanding of either market value or replacement value should be current. This may take some research on your part but this is the only way you can know if this component of the purchase price is reasonable. By listing each item you will guarantee clear communication between you and the seller about what's included. Often she will want the paintings on the wall (grandma gave it to her) and other personal items that you feel will be included in the purchase. I have seen copy machines, computers, and clocks disappear without warning prior to settlement. I often use an addendum that lists items excluded from the purchase because it gives clarification to each party.

Leasehold improvements

If the business operates from rented space there might be a significant number of physical changes in the space that were made specifically for the business. There is a value associated with these improvements, because any operator of this type of business would need to make these improvements to operate a similar business. Special lighting, public restrooms, special plumbing requirements, unusual electrical systems, walls, and the like are generally considered leasehold improvements. If you plan to move the business, you do not want to pay for this value. In fact, you need to budget the improvements in some other space. A landlord sometimes puts a clause in the lease that you will have to restore the premises to the original condition when the lease terminates. Do not get caught in a position where you have to pay for this expensive (and sometimes unnecessary) operation. If the lease needs to be terminated, make the termination the seller's responsibility. Again, the seller already has a relationship with the landlord. You don't need to negotiate with him, too.

Trade fixtures

This includes any item that can be removed by the business owner without subtracting from the real property or leasehold. It may be clearly attached to the premises, yet the Uniform Commercial Code (UCC), valid in all fifty states, allows it to be removed. Check the lease to be sure that the trade fixtures were not supplied by the landlord and therefore belong to him. There may be a cost to repair the premises upon removal if the lease requires it and if you plan to remove it. Trade fixtures also include a variety of items you might normally miss when doing an inventory, such as signs, signposts, shelving, cases, and counters.

Patents and rights

Determine all the rights you will need to continue the operation and make sure they are included in the price and listed in the contract. In a manufacturing business you might need assignment of the patents. In a franchised business you need to purchase the franchise rights and may have to qualify and be acceptable to the franchisor. In retail sales you might need to verify that you will retain distribution rights and area protection from competitors. This matter can be expanded by considering necessary permits and licenses, which may or may not be transferable.

Personalty

The seller may be including some personal property that you are not aware of. By asking him to list all personalty included in the sale you will be sure of what you're buying. If you do not wish to purchase certain items, negotiate. Try not to nit-pick, as you will learn that price and terms are much more important than exactly what the purchase includes. Some sellers just want out. If you make it too difficult, you can send them scurrying to some other buyer (even at a lesser price). Personalty is discussed in greater detail in chapter 8.

Ongoing advertising

By requesting a listing of all ongoing advertising programs, you can check each program to determine if there will be any liability for payment and who will make that payment. It is also a good way to learn what the seller has done in this area before firming up the offering price.

Systems

Depending on the type of business being purchased, there will be certain systems in place that should be part of the sale. Some of them are security systems, cash registers, computers, packaging apparatus, and so forth. Check each system to be sure it is actually owned free and clear. There may be lease or lease/purchase contracts in force and you need to know this. If they are leased or subject to lease/purchase, determine the true and final cost on each item. One way to do this is to ask the leasing company for a buyout price based on the day of settlement. Compare this price with the outright purchase of similar systems. If the cost of purchasing is less, you cannot afford to pay a premium to the seller. Business owners often get into bad lease or lease/purchase agreements to avoid putting out substantial sums of cash. Don't inherit these problems.

street~smarts

Don't Forget the UCC Search
As a piece of real property is subject to a title search, systems and equipment and sometimes inventories are subject to a UCC search. If you place a lien or notice against a business system or equipment, the way to give constructive notice of your lien is by filing under the UCC. This filing serves as a public notice of the lien, and title to the assets filed against should not be transferred without contacting the filers. If you take title without the UCC search, you may wind up without any title at all. Your attorney can arrange for this to be done.

VALUATION OF ASSETS

Having already discussed the quantity and quality of assets that should be included in the purchase of a business, the problem of how to affix a value to these assets remains. There is also a question as to who will calculate the value. It is most desirable to use a neutral third party to conduct the evaluation. There are firms that will come to the place of business and list all the assets, including saleable merchandise. For each classification of business there is a separate class of experts. Try to find an expert through trade associations and the like. Be careful to choose a party who is, in fact, neutral. It is usually not wise to ask the supplier about current value of the items. Since they have sold merchandise to the seller they might not readily admit it is now obsolete. If the seller would offer you the opportunity to sell an asset back to them, you could probably trust the amount they would offer you as being the fair value. Try this and see what happens.

Book value: seller

The seller has a book value placed on all assets. Basically, this is his initial cost of the asset, reduced by depreciation amounts he has taken as an expense against income on the business tax returns. Keep in mind that this may not be your book value, as your accountant will want to set up your books. Your value will be derived from the amount you pay for the assets. If the seller's book value appears to be advantageous to you, there is nothing wrong with using it for the purpose of determining the sales price. If he has used actual cost and you only buy the assets you want, you may make a shrewd purchase in times of inflation. If he is willing to sell at depreciated values, and I have seen this occur, you may make

out very well. The values you use may have tax consequences. Be sure to use the services of a competent accountant who specializes in small businesses.

Book value: buyer

Once your purchase is complete, your accountant will establish book values for the purchased assets. This is an extremely important area of decision-making. Some assets will be depreciated for tax purposes and others may be completely deductible in the first year of operation. The seller's depreciation schedules are meaningless to you unless you purchase an ongoing corporation. Assets need to be separated into classes for depreciation purposes. They will be depreciated over varying numbers of years. Your purchase price will be allocated among the various components of the sale, including the assets. The values you set for saleable merchandise will be your basis for profit and loss calculations when they are sold.

The noncompete agreement

Part of your purchase price may pay for an agreement with the seller not to compete with your newly purchased business. Imagine a new business owner's surprise when the seller opens a new shop across the street! She knows all of your customers and all of your weaknesses. She is in an ideal situation to give you an Excedrin Headache! You may have heard that such agreements are not enforceable in court, but this is not true. Courts have found that if the agreements are reasonable in scope and geography, they are enforceable. An attorney familiar with this type of agreement should be consulted. The noncompete agreement can be amortized over the life of the agreement for tax purposes. If, for example, you pay twenty thousand dollars for an agreement that gives you five years of protection, you may deduct (amortize) four thousand dollars a year from your taxable income. The valuation of this agreement is an important component of your purchase price and should be determined by tax counsel. The amount chosen must be considered reasonable by the IRS.

Depreciation vs. amortization

There is the real world; then there is the tax world. In the tax world, costs, expenses, and assets are placed in specific categories. There is very little choice in this area. Most of it is very specifically categorized by the IRS tax code. When you depreciate an item you deduct a mathematically calculated portion of the cost each year. Theoretically, this allows you to set up a fund for replacement of the item at the end of its useful life. Buildings, furniture, fixtures, and the like are depreciable items. Land is not depreciable. To arrive at the basis for depreciation, you take the cost and subtract from it the expected salvage value at the end of the depreciation period. When you sell an item that has been depreciated, that is to say you have claimed a portion every year as an expense (and received tax benefit from doing so), you must pay income taxes on the amount considered as taxable gain. The basis of the item is reduced each year as you claim depreciation expense. The reduced amount is called your *book value*. Subtract your book value from the amount received in the sale to calculate the taxable gain. These gains are capital gains and may be subject to special tax treatment. The amortized items are ultimately reduced to a zero value and generally are not saleable. Consult your accountant on these matters.

Capitalization vs. expensing

The cost of certain items can be deducted from receipts in the calculation of taxable income for that year. They are said to be *expensed*. The current IRS laws allow you to expense a small amount of equipment and the like annually as the equipment is placed into service. The term *placed into service* is not the same as *when purchased*. If you purchase an automobile on December 31, but do not take delivery until January, the auto cannot be depreciated until January, as it was not placed into service until then. Items that are not allowable as expenses are *capitalized*. Generally, capital assets bring use or benefits to the business over a period of time longer than the tax year.

Allocation of the purchase price

This is an area often overlooked when purchasing a business, but it is extremely important to you. Say you pay $100,000 for a business. What part of the purchase price is allocated toward what assets? The values might be completely different for a buyer and a seller. You would want to pay more for the assets that could be recovered more quickly through amortization or direct expensing. The seller would want to allocate the purchase price to avoid taxable gains on his book values of assets. Again, the advice of competent tax counsel is needed here.

street~smarts

"Location, location, location." This slogan has been around for a long time and it still works. Choosing the site to run your business is of paramount importance. For retailing, you want to be centrally located to the area in which your customers live or work. For service businesses, you hope to be visible (a form of advertising) but it is more important to be centrally located in the area you choose to serve. For manufacturing businesses you need to consider availability of materials, a good labor market, and transportation. If you are selling a business that is in the wrong location, it might pay to move before you sell. If you are buying a business in the wrong location, you might plan to move as part of the purchase.

Many business purchasers have set up their own books after settlement on their new business without regard to the seller's treatment of the purchase price. Should the IRS audit either one of you, they will expect the same treatment by both of you. The time to choose treatment of this allocation or prorating is when you are still in the process of negotiating with the seller. It could affect the purchase price but is too important to overlook or ignore.

GOODWILL: EXCESS OVER BASIS

Often part of the purchase price is paid for *goodwill*. You may have heard it said that goodwill is no longer valid but, again, this is not true. To understand what this value is you need to understand *excess over basis* — which means the amount of purchase price you paid over and above the value of all the assets you are purchasing. Should you pay more than the value of the assets? It is possible to do so and still make a wise purchase. The value of an ongoing business is really its ability to generate income. There are some businesses, service businesses especially, that have few assets, yet generate a lot of income. A buyer usually will pay some amount of goodwill when purchasing one of these businesses. Bankers do not like to hear of or see goodwill. Then again, many bankers have never been in business for themselves and have no practical understanding of its many aspects. Discuss the tax treatment of goodwill with your tax counsel.

When buying a business you want to be careful to leave the seller her dignity in any offer. Even in a distress situation you can

street~smarts

Win-Win Strategy
It's about people. Years ago a business person was considered successful if they could beat the others. Of course if you beat the others and sacrifice the relationships you need to continue in business — you lose. A more successful approach is to structure every transaction or sale so that everybody wins. A good product. A fair price. Treatment with dignity.

be part of the seller's solution. You don't have to overpay to help the seller. You might hire them back for a period to give them some more money. You might offer some consideration other than money if the situation shows a need. You might structure an offer that actually allows the seller to choose from alternatives. For example, you might offer "$100,000 price with no money down or $75,000 cash in sixty days — to be selected and initialed by the seller." The seller decides which option to choose, which becomes part of the contract when he places his initials by the chosen option.

Which of These Items Do You Need Help With?

CHAPTER 6 COMFORT ZONE CHECKLIST

If this book is a library copy, please do not write in it. Photocopy this page instead.

Circle the comfort level for each issue.	High			Low	
I have determined my goals	5	4	3	2	1
I have examined the alternatives	5	4	3	2	1
I have hired the professionals I need	5	4	3	2	1
I checked with my attorney	5	4	3	2	1
I have studied the following information:					
Seller's reasons for selling	5	4	3	2	1
Past sales figures	5	4	3	2	1
Reconstructed profit and loss statement	5	4	3	2	1
Current rents and lease terms	5	4	3	2	1
Fixed overhead costs	5	4	3	2	1
Payroll information	5	4	3	2	1
I am comfortable with:					
Preparing the offer	5	4	3	2	1
Presenting the offer	5	4	3	2	1
Timing of the offer	5	4	3	2	1
What assets to buy	5	4	3	2	1
Inventory and equipment	5	4	3	2	1

Checklist continued on the next page.

Which of these items do you need help with?

If this book is a library copy, please do not write in it. Photocopy this page instead.

Checklist continued from the previous page

Circle the comfort level for each issue.	High			Low	
I am comfortable with:					
Furniture and fixtures	5	4	3	2	1
Leasehold improvements	5	4	3	2	1
Ongoing advertising	5	4	3	2	1
Current systems in working order	5	4	3	2	1
UCC Search	5	4	3	2	1
Valuation of assets	5	4	3	2	1
Trade fixtures	5	4	3	2	1
Personal items	5	4	3	2	1
Patents and rights	5	4	3	2	1
Noncompete agreement	5	4	3	2	1
New business form and tax structure	5	4	3	2	1
Allocation of purchase price	5	4	3	2	1
Goodwill Win-Win strategy	5	4	3	2	1

About your answers: There are no right or wrong answers. Study your responses to determine which items you need help with. Have your spouse or potential partner(s) fill in a copy of the checklist also. Discovering which subjects lack high comfort levels will help you choose professionals with the appropriate skills.

"The simple believeth every word:
but the prudent man looketh well to his going."

Selling your Business

- Determine your Goals and
  Check Alternatives
- Hire a Professional
- Check with your Accountant
- Check with your Lawyer
- Confidential Treatment
- Time Frame Can Be Critical
- Make your Own Decisions
- Mechanics of a Sale
- Packaging
- Telling the Employees
- Telling the Customers
- Telling the Creditors
- Advertising
- Foreign Buyers

Selling a business is not a science — it is an art. While it involves a host of details and transaction steps, the key word is *sell*. What does it take to make a sale? Perhaps the best definition I've heard of selling is to find a need and then fill it. During the entire process of selling your business, you would be wise to focus on the selling aspect of the transaction. Businesses do not sell themselves. People buy from people. When choosing professionals that will assist you in the sale of your business, pay close attention to their people skills as well as their particular area of expertise.

DETERMINE YOUR GOALS AND CHECK ALTERNATIVES

The sale of your business is a real commitment. Before you decide to do so, take the time (away from your business) to cautiously consider the matter. Perhaps you have been approached by an eager purchaser with an offer you can't refuse. I usually challenge my clients to consider what they will do with the money once they sell. Also, I ask them to determine what they will do with their time. I know several business owners who retired early by selling a successful business. Two had heart attacks and one suffered a stroke. Interestingly enough, their doctors all had the same prescription: *Get back to Work!* Just to survive, You need to have something meaningful in life to do. You may choose to volunteer with a local charity. Take an interesting job whether you need the money or not, pursue additional education, or focus on an interesting hobby. Make sure that you have enough money from the sale of your business to accomplish the goals you have decided on. Many sellers find their money doesn't go as far as they thought it would. They discover that while they have been toiling at their business many things have changed. Make sure you haven't been so busy that you've lost touch with the rest of the world!

HIRE A PROFESSIONAL

There are seasoned professionals who can provide valuable counsel to business sellers. If you feel you need this kind of help, here are some pointers to make it easier. Many people offer services in this field but many are not competent. In many states, no license is required to counsel buyers or sellers of businesses. In California, for example, a real estate license is required, but no instruction or courses about business are required. A good professional is hard to find. The following outline should help you with the basic selection process. The person you select should display all of these characteristics.

A numbers man

Although the sale of a business is more than numbers, composing a sales price and the prospective purchaser's need for financing require your professional to be absolutely comfortable with numbers. She should understand present and future values, discounting of income streams, basic taxation, and be *streetwise* about small businesses. Undoubtedly, he or she will have some formal education. This might be a degree in business, preferably with accounting or finance as a major, and considerable business experience. An accountant's expertise is not sufficient unless their sole practice is counseling in buying and selling of businesses.

You need someone who has demonstrated success in marketing, preferably well-connected with various buyers' markets. A real estate specialist in the field of businesses with the designation of *CCIM* would be a real find. A CCIM is a Certified Commercial Investment Member. This individual has completed a series of post-graduate courses about commercial real estate and investment, has been tested for proficiency in use of the studies, and demonstrated capability through a certain volume or number of completed transactions. The CCIM designee is considered the Ph.D. of commercial real estate. As with any professional, discuss fees up front. Do not be anxious to fund a lot of marketing and advertising dollars, especially if you want your offer to sell kept in strict confidence.

A good negotiator

Your professional should be better at negotiating than you. If he will represent you with prospective buyers, many opportunities will arise for his negotiating skills. Remember, you will freely discuss your goals with this person. Their job will be to help you achieve those goals. A professional should be able to guide a prospective purchaser to make an intelligent offer. The statement "I don't believe his attorney will allow that" can keep unreasonable demands out of offers, even before they are presented. Your professional should be well-versed in the area's demographics and in the market in which your business specializes. He will know how to wield facts and figures that benefit his presentation on your behalf.

A practical businessperson

There is no greater danger than an intelligent person who has no practical street experience. Some things look so good on paper, yet do not make any real sense when you put them into practice. Remember my college professor who said, "This is the input data — what do you want me to prove?" This turned out to be one of my favorite classes. A practical professional has had enough experience in the business world to keep you out of trouble. This person should have operated one or more small businesses by themselves. Whether it was greatly successful or not is of no real consequence.

A paralegal

You don't really need a paralegal of course, but your professional should be very comfortable with the legal structure of a sale and the related contract forms. Ask to see the forms this individual would use if you agree to hire her. A wrong word on your contract of sale could constitute an improper representation on your part. You are more likely to wind up in court than your advisor, so hire someone you are confident will help keep you out of trouble and add real value in the sale process.

Good marketing skills

A good way to understand your broker's capabilities is to ask him for a marketing plan. How does he plan to market your business? When and where will he advertise? Will he screen prospects to eliminate those that do not qualify financially? To what networks will he expose your business opportunity? What level of commitment can you expect? Write down the questions important to you for the interview. Listen carefully to the answers. The professional must gain your confidence if he is to gain the confidence of others. A good broker will furnish a marketing plan outline before you hire him.

Ask for references

Don't be his training ground. I can't think of a more important step in hiring an individual than talking with people who have already done business with him. Take for granted that the list of references furnished may be his favorite clients. Make a list of questions you plan to ask each reference. What are the broker's strong points? Weak points? How often did the two of you communicate? Were the communications clear? Did he achieve the goals for which he were hired? Was he able to produce prospects in a timely manner? Did he screen the prospects? Did he advertise? When and where?

Ask for personal references as well. If the references you receive have nothing to do with buying or selling businesses, keep looking. The personal references should likewise be from the list of clients he has helped. Request a list of ten. Would you use him again? Do you have any particular advice for me in selling my business? Was all information was kept confidential?

Businesses for sale should not be openly advertised. Suppliers could limit your credit. Employees might be overcautious about the prospects of a new owner and leave your employ. Banks have been known to call loans in early. Competitors should not know of your desire for a sale unless they are really potential purchasers. By checking references you want to ensure your candidate is effective, honest, and confidential.

Discuss fees

The cheapest might not be the best. There is no set fee for a professional's services. Some work on commission. Some will quote a specific fee. Some have a minimum fee. Some may seek to charge you administrative or packaging fees. Others may ask you to pay for any advertising. Again, the interview process is an excellent time to negotiate the fees. Document the expectations both for fees and services. This is usually done in the form of a listing or representation agreement. Don't be in a hurry to sign this. It will be a contract between you and the professional. Make sure that every representation made verbally appears in print. Of course, you are most interested in the bottom line. What will you have left after paying the fees? You must remember that buyers are paying one price. They generally have no obligation to pay fees. This means that a higher fee will necessitate a higher sales price for your business. On the other hand, you may not want to hire the least expensive professional unless you are fairly certain he can get the job done. Like any other thing for sale, potential buyers may perceive your business as stale if it stays on the market too long.

Pay attention to the time period for which you will be obligated to the professional. Many agreements are for a one-year period. Some will allow you to cancel after a number of months provided you give notice in writing that you wish to cancel. You should give the professional enough time to get the word out and expose your business to each of his networks. However, you may have time constraints or pressures that require a quick sale. Discuss them with the professional. Understand that a quick sale or any form of perceived distress will most likely reduce the dollar amount of offers.

CHECK WITH YOUR ACCOUNTANT

Your accountant should know your complete financial condition. Will the net proceeds of a sale be enough to accomplish your goals in the selling of your business? What taxes will you need to pay? What is your basis in the business? How much of a potential sale will be a recapture of depreciation or amortization? Your accountant should help you understand how much of the sale proceeds you can expect to hold onto.

What is your cash position? Can you afford to offer sensible seller financing? (You will generally achieve a higher sales price if you do.) What liabilities must be paid from the sale proceeds?

What is your borrowing power? Your accountant may have some ideas that you have not yet thought of. Would it be a good idea for you to refinance your business instead of selling? Could you sell to a competent employee, business acquaintance, or a competitor? Can your accountant offer some ideas to restructure your business that would enhance the saleability?

Your accountant should review all numbers and figures that will be used in any presentation of your business for sale. Because of the potential litigation that can arise from alleged misrepresentations, it is wise to have the third party involved. If possible, it is even better to have your accountant prepare or verify numbers, figures, and projections.

Your accountant is a professional. Therefore, discuss the fees for his consultation in advance.

CHECK WITH YOUR LAWYER

Frankly, if every lawyer were a good businessperson they probably wouldn't have time for you. Never let your lawyer make your business decisions. You want her to check everything for legal sufficiency and look for potential problems that may give rise to litigation. She may wish to write the sales agreement but that would probably cost thousands of dollars. In my business practice I have found it better to receive the offer from a buyer and then check it for legal sufficiency and review it for legal pitfalls. I would suggest that all the terms and conditions be agreed upon before taking the document to counsel. Of course, I wouldn't sign anything until it was reviewed by counsel.

CONFIDENTIAL TREATMENT

One of the worst things that can happen to a business is having employees find out that it is for sale. For some reason they always expect the worst. They will not want to work with the new owner. They fear that the new

street~smarts

Did I mention the power lunch? Invite your legal professional to lunch. At that time, ask how much he or she would charge to check a five-page (or seven-page) sales document for legal sufficiency. Just happen to have the document with you. This is in line with my advice to discuss fees in advance. Believe it or not, sometimes lunch will do!

owner will bring his family into the operation and fire the existing employees. With this attitude, they might quit and take employment elsewhere. If you suspect that this may happen in your business, discuss the matter when you interview the professionals. It is difficult to market a business without disclosing the actual location and nature of the business. Not impossible. Some professionals use a confidentiality statement. Unless a prospective purchaser is willing to agree to keep all information confidential, the information is not released to him.

If you want the world to know your business is for sale (including your competitors) tell your professional you expect prominent advertising. I once placed a "For Sale" sign in the window of a business — it sold to one of the customers! If you are not sure what to do, then keep it confidential.

dollars by creating the perception that you are in distress.

TIME FRAME CAN BE CRITICAL

Once you decide to sell your business you may feel instant relief. Put those feelings on hold. You need to keep your concentration focused on operating your business. You must operate your business as if you will be there forever — especially during the period of time your business is being marketed. If a prospect comes to look at your business, you want them to see it at its best.

Not even the best professional would be willing to tell you how long it will take to sell your business. The longer it takes to sell — the more frustrated you can get. It will be easy to let this frustration pour over into your personal life and also affect your business. As time goes on, you will need to make decisions regarding your asking price. Is the price too high? If you've had several prospects inspect the books and records but not make offers, it might be the price. But if no prospects have been found, there is no reason to suspect that price is a factor. Remember the marketing plan you received from your professional. If the process is moving too slowly give her a call and discuss the matter. Remember it's the squeaky hinge that gets oiled. On the other hand, if you are pushing for a quick sale, it can cost many

MAKE YOUR OWN DECISIONS

Once a prospect has been secured, your professional should take responsibility for making sure all the necessary information is conveyed to him. Once this has been done, it is soon decision time. No amount of coaching can prepare you for this part of the sale. You cannot let anybody make your decisions for you — not your lawyer, not your accountant, and certainly not your professional. It is fine to solicit opinions from every source possible, but you will still have to make your own decisions. Some will be tough. You may risk losing a sale when you negotiate. Determine in advance where your bottom line is, and don't tell anyone. Remember your goals for the sale of your business and make sure you achieve them. Never let anyone pressure you into making a decision until you have thoroughly investigated the details. Do not sign any document until it has undergone legal review. In the end, the best decisions are made from the pit of your stomach. If you have good decision-making skills you will do well in business. If not, trusting others to make decisions for you will not make your skills better.

MECHANICS OF A SALE

The mechanics of the sale are the reverse of the mechanics involved in purchasing a business. They are explained in detail in chapter 6. You can use the strategies for buying a business to your advantage by structuring your sale to accommodate purchasers. The buyer wants a good cash flow. Structure the sale to include a direct purchase of all the equipment you lease. The cash flow of the business will improve. If the business has an excellent cash flow you may consider leasing some of your equipment, which will effectively reduce the purchaser's need for capital.

PACKAGING

Hopefully, your professional will be better at this than you are. But don't be so sure. You need to approve of any and all materials used in marketing your business. Here are some pointers for structuring or reviewing your sales package. Ask yourself these questions: What will others want to see (or prove)? What information can I show? Sales, rents, payroll? What information should I withhold? Balance Sheet? What about the confidentiality statement requirement?

Consider making these part of your sales package:

- Pictures
- Location map
- Industry averages price list
- Menu
- Key employees/bios
- Sales by month
- Sales brochures
- Equipment list
- Hours of operation
- History of business
- Product lists
- Competitive advantages
- Real estate description and/or details of leasehold
- Notes about opportunities to improve your business. (What changes would you make if you were just buying this business?)

ADVERTISING

Should you advertise the sale of your business? Tough question. If you are a bed and breakfast the answer is easy. Yes. Advertise in the periodicals that are devoted to bed and breakfast owners. In general, trade publications are effective for specific industries. You might want to tell your trusted suppliers. Tell the salespeople and it will be all over town in less than a week! Sometimes that's good. You might consider competitors from outside the area. Many business grow by acquisition. It can be a good way to obtain solid management and trained employees. With the counsel of your professional, plan the advertising campaign that you believe will work. Be sensitive to your situation.

FOREIGN BUYERS

Many people are coming to the United States from foreign countries and are looking for businesses to purchase and operate. In some cases, providing a job for relatives in the United States will allow that relative to come here and enjoy the freedom of this country. (The money they pay you with is U.S. dollars). How do you reach this population? Look for newspapers, radio stations, clubs, and churches that serve those demographics. If you are having difficulty reaching the new American population then call your local newspaper. They have demographic staffs that know where everybody is — and they would love to have some advertising dollars from you.

TELLING THE EMPLOYEES

Although it might be the most honest thing to do, your employees may feel the situation is no longer stable if they know you're trying to sell. They could take jobs elsewhere and that might affect your operation. There is no way you can guarantee that a purchaser will keep the current employees. Slavery has been abolished. So there is no way you can guarantee your employees the stability they want. It may be better to keep the information confidential until you are sure you have found the purchaser. You are never sure you are selling your business until you have found the actual purchaser. Be careful not to rock the boat prematurely.

TELLING THE CUSTOMERS

Who will stand behind the products or services you sell when the new owner takes over? Certainly you hope the new owner will treat your customers the same way you have done, but you cannot be sure. So how can you promise your customers anything? How about businesses that have work in progress? I know of an auto body shop that listed for sale publicly only to be boycotted by the major customers — the insurance industry. They did not want to take the chance that change of ownership would affect the autos that were being repaired under their claims. It almost cost that man his life savings! Each situation is different. You need to decide whether to mention your possible or pending sale to customers, and, if so, what timing is best.

TELLING THE CREDITORS

Your creditors include your suppliers,

lenders, and insurers. A supplier might put you on COD if he learns that your business is for sale. A lender might bring pressures that otherwise would not be expected. An insurer could refuse to extend a policy or benefits if it considered your decision to have a major impact on the stability of your account. Again, each situation is unique. But you must consider whether it is wise to disclose that you are contemplating selling your business. Whether you sell the business or are unable to sell, you would suffer the same consequences with a bad decision.

Are You Prepared to Begin the Sale Process?

Circle the comfort level for each issue.	High			Low	
I have determined my goals	5	4	3	2	1
My professional for hire is/has:					
Honest & confidential	5	4	3	2	1
A good numbers man	5	4	3	2	1
A good negotiator	5	4	3	2	1
A practical businessperson	5	4	3	2	1
A paralegal	5	4	3	2	1
Reviewed the marketing plan	5	4	3	2	1
Good references	5	4	3	2	1
Fees negotiated	5	4	3	2	1
I have:					1
Checked with my accountant	5	4	3	2	1
Checked with my attorney	5	4	3	2	1
Taken steps to ensure confidentiality	5	4	3	2	1
Determineda time frame	5	4	3	2	1
Will make my own decisions	5	4	3	2	1
Ensured the mechanics of sale are structured	5	4	3	2	1
A complete sales package	5	4	3	2	1
Plan to tell employees	5	4	3	2	1
Plan to tell customers/clients	5	4	3	2	1
Plan to tell creditors	5	4	3	2	1
Advertising/marketing plan in place	5	4	3	2	1
Considered reaching foreign buyers	5	4	3	2	1

About your answers: There are no right or wrong answers. Study your responses to determine which items you need help with. Discovering which subjects lack high comfort levels will help you choose professionals with the appropriate skills.

"For wisdom is better than rubies."

Elements of a Business Contract

- Deposits
- Terms
- Supplements
- Resale Merchandise
- Assets to Be Transferred
- Instructions to Attorneys
- Prorations
- Bills of Sale
- Lease Assignment
- Liquor or Other Licenses
- Bulk Sales Requirement
- Books and Records
- Seller's Operation until
   Settlement
- Possession
- Transition Plan
- Liabilities to Be Assumed
   by Buyer
- Sales and Use Taxes
- Liquidated Damages
- Arbitration
- Attorneys' Fees
- Acceptance Time Frame
- Corporate Acknowledgment
   and Acceptance
- Payroll Taxes and Other
   Liabilities
- Due Diligence Time Frame
- Time Is of the Essence

There is no *one* document that is universally acceptable for all potential transactions. Certain states allow business brokers to draft contracts. Other states require a real estate license and that the contracts must be approved or have certain clauses in them. Store-bought contracts are available, but not for the meek! If you hire a professional to help you buy or sell, she should have some good basic forms.

The right form can be one of the best helps in seeing what you're buying or what your obligations could be as a seller. In supplying the information the form requires, the areas of negotiation become more clear. Once price and terms are agreed upon, there are many conditions that need to be addressed.

DEPOSITS

A good decision about the deposit can make or break any transaction. It's not only about the money. It's the psychology of the game — the proof of a buyer's worth and credibility, as well as protection against default. Since the deposit is negotiable, I will present several aspects about deposits for your consideration.

How much should the deposit be?

In residential real estate transactions, many agents feel that five percent of the purchase price is a reasonable down payment or deposit. In the sale or purchase of a business there is no set rule. It's necessary to have a deposit, as a contract is not valid without consideration. It's even nice for a seller to have the chance to see who the buyer banks with and who signs the checks. But the amount is totally negotiable. The buyer will want to put up the minimum deposit. A seller would prefer something substantial at risk to guarantee performance — especially if the seller will take the business off the market during a successful marketing season (multiple offers). Unless the contract

specifies otherwise, the deposit will be money that is forfeited if the buyer does not perform on his obligations. The amount of the deposit is a psychological exercise. If a buyer can impress a seller by his deposit, he has made a certain statement. If a seller demands an unreasonable amount of money at risk, that, too is a certain statement. I prefer to use common sense.

Almost every contract has contingencies that must be met before title or assets change hands. I suggest your contract should allow for these contingencies to be met or waived within a reasonably short period of time — usually a week or two. During the due diligence period, when contingencies are being satisfied, I usually suggest a one thousand dollar deposit. Yes, even on a large transaction. Why such a small amount? Because a reasonable lawyer will not be tempted to litigate to tie up this amount of money. A reasonable seller can walk away from this deposit. A buyer who realizes he has made a default will often walk away from this amount. Once the contingencies are met or waived, the deposit can be increased to demonstrate that the buyer has the cash necessary to perform the contract.

Who holds the deposit?

Convention on this issue varies from state to state and from area to area. It is better for the deposit to be held by someone who is independent of the buyer. It is a good idea for the deposit to be held by someone who is independent of the seller. While I have seen sellers hold the buyer's deposit, this is not a good idea. There is a difference in allowing escrowed funds to be returned and writing a check to return money from your own account.

I shudder when lawyers hold money. Not because I don't trust them with the money. Lawyers and real estate agents/brokers are highly regulated in regard to what they can or cannot do with deposit monies. But all too often I have seen a lawyer intent on earning his fees tie up a deposit and refuse release. Lawyers are not even afraid of litigation like real estate brokers are. Litigation is their game.

The deposit should be held by someone who has a trust account for the purpose of holding deposits that is not in the direct control of either buyer or seller. If there is a broker involved in the transaction, and that broker is regulated, the deposit should placed with her.

Is the deposit forfeitable?

That depends on what is written in the contract. What did the seller do to earn the deposit from the buyer? Did he supply information to the buyer that discouraged the sale? Then he should not be entitled to the deposit. Did the seller really take the property off the market? Or did he continue taking backup offers? If a qualified buyer does not purchase your business you should be wondering why he did not want it — not trying to figure out how to profit from the situation. On many representation agreements the broker is entitled to half of any forfeited deposits. I encourage you to remove that clause from any agreement you sign. I don't want my broker tying up my life while he attempts to retain a deposit that was not really earned.

After all the contingencies are met and/or waived, perhaps with the exception of the funding of any required loans, the deposit should be at risk. The only way to put the deposit at risk is to specify this clearly in the contract.

When will my deposit check be cashed?

It is my hope that anyone who writes a check should expect it to be cashed. This is not always the case. You might be surprised how many times I have heard this: "Call me before you deposit that check." The check needs to be cashed upon acceptance of your offer to purchase. Some sophisticated buyers use letters of credit instead of cash. The proper day-to-day use of cash is constantly changing in our world. Many businesspeople today have mutual fund accounts with check privileges. Others have savings accounts that are companion to their checking account. They may call the bank and transfer funds into checking, or do it at an ATM machine anywhere in the world. In some states, real estate deposits must be cashed, according to state law, at the time the offer is made — not when the offer is accepted.

Under what circumstances will the deposit be returned? Treatment of deposit money is governed by the contract language and by state laws. Most of the state legislation is meant for residential transactions, but you will find one common denominator — if all parties do not agree to the release of the deposit and it is held by someone with a trust/escrow account, it will not be released without court approval. Generally, a fee for the court's review will be deducted from the deposit before the court determines its award. How will the court decide? They will read the contract.

Are any increases in the deposit called for?
Only if it's written in the contract. If it is not in the contract, and you want it in there — write it in. The buyers and sellers are the negotiators. If they understand their powerful roles, they will take responsibility for each and every part of any agreement they sign. Never let brokers, lawyers, or other professionals make you think the decisions are not in your control. Insist on any offer being just what you want. Listen to others' opinions, but then make your own decisions.

TERMS

There is an adage in the brokerage community that says, "Price or terms — choose one." The choice makes sense if you stop to think about it. If the offer is full price, the seller feels he is getting what he wants. But what do the terms look like? The buyer may be asking for one hundred percent seller financing. Inspection periods may be very long. There may be contingencies that may be difficult to satisfy. On the other hand, an all-cash offer may be at a very low price. Such an offer may provide for very little time until settlement and very few contingencies. Which would be the better offer? Much depends on the seller's situation. Either offer may be acceptable to the seller. But generally you do not get both price and terms. Expect one or the other.

SUPPLEMENTS

Besides price and terms there are various issues that need to be addressed in the contract for sale and purchase. These should be considered as *terms* of the contract since they are important, and they may seriously affect the value of an offer. All supplements should be mentioned in the contract of sale and are usually attached to the contract. Both buyer and seller should initial each page of each supplement to show that he or she has read and acknowledges

Price:

One Offer? Or Tennis Anyone?

As a buyer, do you think it's best to make just *one* offer and tell a seller to take it or leave it? As a seller, do you expect this to happen? Or do you think a prudent buyer might make a first offer lower than he was willing to pay?

The art of splitting the difference is still around but don't depend on it. As a buyer, you should realize that buying the right business often doesn't really cost any money. A well-priced business with a good cash flow should pay itself off. Do you want to play games and lose the purchase to another buyer? Do you want to win — or appear to win?

Mr. Seller — if you want to play tennis, reserve a court. Anytime you refuse an offer to purchase you have actually bought the business back at that price. If you pass up a certain price offer and refuse a sale, you lose the ability to control that amount of money. It's like buying your business back, isn't it?

that each supplement is part of the agreement. A good idea is to make sure each supplement is labeled in such a manner that a judge would be sure that it was, in fact, a part of the contract.

Inventory of personal property included

A business will usually have personal property items that are needed to sustain operations. The term *personal property* or *personalty* can easily be misunderstood. For the context of this discussion we will consider anything that is not *real property* as personalty. Items that may or may not be included in a sale will be trade fixtures, furnishings, equipment, office equipment and supplies, computers and systems, security systems, and the like. Any item may be included or excluded in a sale. The important issue is to state clearly which items are included and which are not.

A good way to treat the inclusion or exclusion of personalty is to provide an addendum to the contract that actually lists each personal item that is to be part of the purchase price. The items generally will not have values or prices listed, as the seller's book value is not important to the buyer. The buyer's accountant will later assign values to the personalty which will be depreciated on the buyer's profit and loss statement. As a buyer it would be advantageous to determine the seller's book values since you will get a better look at his equity. This could affect the amount one might offer for the business assets. As a seller you should never offer a balance sheet, as this information has great potential to be misunderstood. How much depreciation you wrote off is really not any of a buyer's business, nor is the amount you actually paid for the personalty. A more appropriate value for these assets would be an estimate of the current market value or replacement value of the assets.

Listing exclusions on a separate addendum adds clarity to the intent of the agreement. Remember to list the personal items you might have in your office, as well as your personal wallhangings and personal computer if these assets are not intended to be part of the sale. An even better idea would be to remove all of the items you intend to exclude before any prospect visits or inspects your business premises. Discuss any items that will be excluded with your professional at the time the asking price of the business is established.

Accounts receivable list

It is generally not a good idea to purchase accounts receivable. Even when purchased at a discount the purchase price is increased and the purchase requires more capital. The collectability of any account is questionable. The risk of collection should stay

street~smarts

Accounts Receivable
A seller may consider the accounts receivable to be part of the business and allow them to convey as part of the business purchase. I counseled one client who was buying a small contracting business to include *all* the assets in his purchase offer. We included the cash in the bank account, inventory, and even the accounts receivable. The receivables were worth more than the price of the business! Part of our performance note seller-financing allowed us to pay the seller thirty-five percent of the receivables, but only upon collection of the amounts. The seller needed out of the business immediately (for health reasons) and was actually satisfied with the arrangement. The transaction met his goal strategy, and my client made a shrewd purchase. Yes — we collected about ninety-two percent of the receivables.

with the seller as he generated the receivable. If it is necessary for the receivables to be involved in the purchase, the buyer may agree to collect the accounts and remit the collections to the seller as received. The buyer should charge some fee or percentage for the collection of such accounts. Using this strategy, the receivables would not have to be purchased by the buyer.

Allocation of purchase price

There are three schools of thought on this matter. When a buyer pays a certain price for the business and the assets, a question arises as to what each individual asset costs. The seller will have one idea, but the buyer may have quite a different idea. The importance of assigning values to assets is how they are treated for tax purposes. Items may either be depreciated or amortized, depending on the asset class to which they are assigned. These classes are mandated according to IRS rules and regulations.

If the seller assigns values to each asset then the buyer must live with the values. In this manner the seller establishes the tax consequences of his sale. This scenario is advantageous to the seller, but it could hurt a sales price to insist on this. If the buyer assigns values to each asset then the seller must live with the values. In this scenario, the buyer is mandating the values that will affect not only her own depreciation and amortization, but also affect the seller's tax consequences of the sale. Clearly this method is favorable to the buyer. She is able to set up advantageous depreciation and amortization schedules to minimize income taxes in the future.

The IRS will not be happy if you don't assign values to assets in the purchase contract. In theory, the buyer and seller can agree on the values after the contract is accepted. In reality, both the buyer and seller could direct their accountants to determine how to allocate the purchase price to the assets being sold/purchased. If the buyer and seller chose different values (and they most likely would) the IRS would frown. An audit of one or both of the parties could raise questions that would be difficult to answer. The IRS would most likely assign the values they felt were appropriate. In such a case, both buyer and seller would have to change their records and be subject to changed tax consequences. On the subject of allocation of purchase price, each party should consult their respective accountant and/or tax attorney.

Copy of the lease

Any business purchase that does not include the purchase of the underlying real estate is probably subject to a lease of some sort. Any purchase contract that involves a lease should require the offer to be subject to a legal review of the lease document.

According to the terms of the lease, it may not be assignable to a new tenant. There may not be enough time left on a lease for the buyer to recover his investment before the need to relocate. A lease may not exist. If you wish to negotiate with a property owner for a lease extension or renewal options, wouldn't you rather do this before buying the business?

One of the dangers of choosing the professional who will help you market your business is that many of them are not licensed real estate agents or brokers. They may have little or no knowledge about leases or lease terms or conditions. They are not permitted by law to be involved in this part of the transaction. This could prove to be expensive for either the buyer or the seller. One wrong assumption, or a piece of bad advice, could give rise to expensive litigation and damage or disappointment to one or all parties to the transaction.

Noncompete agreement

Would you be angry if you purchased someone's business only to find them open a new business across the street and all their loyal customers follow them? I'm sure you would. That is why you want a promise from the seller that he will not do so. The instrument is called the *noncompete agreement* or *covenant not to compete*. If the agreement is so restrictive that a court finds it could de-

prive the seller of making a living, the court could set this promise aside. The agreement must be reasonable within the eyes of the law. If an agreement is "within the same industry/trade within a five-mile radius for a period of five years" chances are it will be considered "reasonable." An attorney might help you feel comfortable with the language to accept.

Some buyers would rather pay for a covenant not to compete rather than for other assets, such as goodwill. Why? They can amortize the cost of the covenant over the life of the covenant. If you can write off an amount over five years instead of seven years or longer, you can reduce income taxes in the earlier years.

Copies of any contracts, warranties, etc.

An offer should be subject to review of documents such as contracts and warranties. One way to keep these items out of the contract would be to supply them to the buyer in advance of the acceptance of the contract. The seller needs to disclose and the buyer needs to know the existence of any leases and/or contracts for which the buyer will be liable. The seller will not want to continue to be liable for the contracts or leases either, but that is a different matter. Never assume liabilities cease when you sell a business. Have everything covered in the contract of sale and know for sure before you sign it.

Lists of suppliers and customers

A prudent seller will usually not be willing to give this type of information before an offer (with a deposit) is accepted. One reason is that the buyer would have potentially damaging information if she did not go through with the purchase. This information often has a real value to a business being purchased, but is not always treated as valuable information.

RESALE MERCHANDISE

This is normally called *inventory* and is usually added to the purchase price for the business. Inventory should be purchased at cost only. It does not make sense to pay retail for items you will need to make a profit on to survive in the business. Not everyone has the same understanding of inventory however, so it should be clearly labeled in the purchase contract.

Inventory cannot be depreciated as part of the purchase price. Inventory cannot be deducted by a purchaser except as an offset to actual sales. Not all inventory is worth purchasing. A prudent buyer would exclude any unsaleable inventory, which would include outdated, damaged, or undesirable items. If the value of the inventory cannot be clearly established by a seller, you can hire an independent firm to tabulate the value of the inventory. The value of

the inventory should be calculated at or immediately prior to transfer of ownership of the business.

A purchase contract should provide for the seller to continue to operate the business in substantially the same manner as done prior to the acceptance of a purchase contract. The contract should limit the seller's ability to reduce the inventory to undesirable limits prior to settlement. In the unusual event that inventory is included in the purchase price you may find the seller will attempt to increase his yield from the sale by reducing the inventory, but the quality of the business would likely suffer.

If it is determined that inventory levels are higher than desired by the purchaser, or that some of the inventory is not desired, it should be the responsibility of the seller to dispose of such unwanted inventory items. He has several options for disposing of these items: return them to the suppliers for refund or credit; have an inventory reduction sale; or trash them. A selling price will be more honest if it does not include items that appear to have value to a seller but have no real value to a buyer.

ASSETS TO BE TRANSFERRED

List all assets to be transferred. These assets can include work in progress, leasehold improvements, telephone numbers, customer lists, trade names, signs, all transferable permits, franchise rights, and customer deposits. Bills of sale will be required to prove ownership in the future. Check state laws to determine whether sales or other taxes will be required upon transfer.

INSTRUCTIONS TO ATTORNEYS

If you agree to any special terms and conditions that will be prepared and/or handled by others, be sure that specific and clear instructions are in the contract. One party's attorney will be checking to be sure all employment taxes are paid to-date. An attorney will also make sure no financial encumbrances are filed against the assets and check similar matters. Instruct them when to settle and how to handle the escrowed funds.

PRORATIONS

This part of the contract of sale divides the ongoing costs of the business between the buyer and seller. Examples are rents, utilities, advertising, and the like. There is no set formula for dividing these costs, though they will be treated in "the normal manner" by attorneys if you do not specify a method or formula in the contract. Items that should be included in the list of prorations are property taxes, rents, in-

terests, insurance (acceptable to buyer and approved by the insurer), and prepaid deposits. A shrewd seller might insist on the buyer paying all costs, but the buyer may not agree to these terms. The net effect of how these costs are handled will be more or less money in someone's pocket.

BILLS OF SALE

The form is not as important as the requirement for the seller to execute the bills of sale. These bills will provide proof of ownership to the assets listed.

LEASE ASSIGNMENT

Another important part of the contract will be an assignment of the lease rights. This assignment is usually with the written consent of the landlord. Courts have generally held that a landlord may not unreasonably withhold consent to an assignment. One method of determining what is *reasonable* is that a new tenant's net worth equals or exceeds the net worth of the tenant wishing to assign the lease. If both parties are strong tenants this requirement would most likely not apply. If you are having trouble getting permission to assign a lease (or take assignment) you should involve your attorney.

LIQUOR OR OTHER LICENSES

Not all licenses are transferable. Some have requirements that must be met such as one-year residency in the state. Be sure to check the possibility of transfer before entering into a contract. State in the contract who will pay the costs of transfer. Again, there is no set formula. Negotiate.

BULK SALES REQUIREMENT

There may be a state requirement for you to do a *bulk sales transfer*. This is a procedure in which you advertise to the public that you are selling your business and advise creditors that they must contact you by a certain date if you owe them money. A creditor can lose rights to collect in certain circumstances if she fails to contact you. As a buyer you want to be sure that the seller does the advertising. You want to make sure you have a defense against any creditors of the former owner's business. Some states will be part of the process and will levy a tax against the assets being sold/purchased.

BOOKS AND RECORDS

One area of buying or selling a business that generates a great deal of litigation is through misunderstandings and/or misrepresentations about books and records. Certainly, a buyer wants to know what the income and expenses are for the business he is about to buy. A seller who wants a decent price will supply enough information to the buyer to enable him to make a decision about the health and potential of the business. So far everything seems reasonable. Your job is to keep it that way. You want to avoid litigation.

Here is a good way to proceed. The contract should state that the seller will furnish all records requested within a specific time period (perhaps seven days). The buyer will then have (according to the contract) a reasonable time to review the records (perhaps another seven days from receipt of same) and make a determination whether to proceed with the sale or not. If the buyer does not respond to the seller within the prescribed time frame that he is not satisfied with the results of his review, then the contingency for books and records is waived.

What records might a buyer request? Sales figures and expenses are most important. With these two items one could reconstruct a profit and loss statement, perhaps with some anticipated changes. Sales figures might be by the month for the past thirty-six months and by categories. Expenses might include noncash tax items such as depreciation and personal expenses of the seller that you might not have to pay. Look for these items as they may distort the actual profitability and cash flow of the business.

A seller should offer as little information as possible (within reason). Too much detail gives rise to too many questions. It is usual for buyers to ask for tax returns for the business, and the figures must match the ones you supply on profit and loss statements. Sellers sometimes refuse to allow buyers to see the tax returns. This will have a negative impact on price since the buyer will probably make financial adjustments to his own projections. The buyer should ask for all the information he feels should be available. The buyer is making an important decision and will be hesitant if he does not receive what he asks for. Your accountant can take the barest of details and provide you with projections of what the business should be doing. She will want sales, rents, cost of sales, and payroll costs. She doesn't actually need all those items though; there is so much historic data on similar businesses across the nation that she can make close estimates based on sales, payroll, and rents only.

A seller (or his professional) may make statements or suggestions that not all the money received goes into the cash register. Ignore him. The only income you can consider is the income shown on the tax returns. If there is any question about the level of income or sales, a buyer may wish to work in the business for a week or two as a condition of the contract. Work near or at the cash register or in a position that records in-

come and prepares deposits for the business. After a few weeks there shouldn't be any question left about income.

Verify any and all records provided by the seller in any manner you can. Ask for additional documentation if there is any question. Ask the seller how he might resolve your issues and see what ideas he might have.

SELLER'S OPERATION UNTIL SETTLEMENT

There should be a clause in your contract that requires the seller to operate the business diligently and substantially in the same manner prior to the sale until the settlement date. The seller should not be able to change hours, labor schedules, prices, and the like during the period of the contract.

The results of such changes could materially affect the value of the business.

POSSESSION

The seller should resist all temptations to turn the business over to a buyer prior to settlement, transfer of the assets, and full payment of the price. You might be surprised how often this is requested by buyers. A seller would not want to be responsible for any detrimental actions of the buyer. Think of some of the consequences. What would happen if the buyer's financing falls through, or is not approved or funded? What would happen if the buyer treats key employees poorly and they quit? What would happen if the buyer is so lacking in experience that she makes poor decisions in every phase of the business? The list of potential liabilities goes on.

TRANSITION PLAN

Most business sale and purchase transactions provide for an orderly transition from the seller to the buyer, and for some period of time after the sale is consummated. It is not unusual for the seller to offer training to the buyer for a period of up to six months. Smart sellers demand compensation for the hours put in during the training and help. Even if a shrewd buyer was able to con-

street~smarts

The Three Things

Be sure to ask any seller what three things he could do to make the business even better. Never assume that a business owner is doing all they can to make the business better — especially if the business is for sale. The seller may be tired. The seller may not have sufficient capital to make desired changes. However, they are in the best position to suggest changes or improvements. They know the business. They have actual experience with the specific business. You don't have to implement any of the ideas offered, but it doesn't hurt to ask.

tract for free help, what would happen to the seller's motivation to show up at the shop? Nothing for nothing! I always try to negotiate a win-win in this area. I suggest reasonable compensation during the training (not included in the lower purchase price), a clear outline of the hours to be worked and the duties to be performed during the training period, and usually have the seller serve at will according to the buyer's desires. If it doesn't work out, the buyer notifies the seller that the training is at an end. So is the compensation.

LIABILITIES TO BE ASSUMED BY BUYER
Although the ideal situation is that a buyer pays all cash and the seller hands over the keys to the place of business, this does not happen all the time. Buyers do not always have all the capital they need to give you all the cash you want. A seller could loan some money to the buyer and ask for security other than the business (such as a second mortgage on his residence). Or a buyer might promise to assume certain liabilities of the business so the seller does not have to pay for them. Use great caution in such a matter. Creditors are not so foolish as to let you off the hook automatically. Try to get the buyer to take the liability in his own name and get a release from the creditor. If that doesn't work try to get the creditor to grant credit to the buyer and offer to pay only if the buyer fails to pay. In essence, you will be guaranteeing the repayment. In such an event look for additional collateral from the buyer.

SALES AND USE TAXES
In states that have sales or use taxes a buyer must ensure that the seller's tax liabilities have been paid. Since some tax liabilities

cannot be calculated until the business transfers, your attorney can escrow an amount of money that should be reasonably expected to satisfy the taxes to be due. Taxing entities will try to collect taxes owed by the business from a new owner if they are not paid by the previous owner. Don't take the chance.

LIQUIDATED DAMAGES
If a contract fails to go forward, what happens? You can't know for sure. Once lawyers get involved it can get very expensive. It would be wise to have a clause in your contract that specifies an amount of money to be considered as *liquidated damages*. This amount of money specified will be accepted by both parties as full settlement when forfeited. After the acceptance of the money forfeited, neither party will have any obligation to the other under the contract. Of course, this is only if it is specified clearly in the contract. Since the amount of money usually chosen for liquidated damages is the deposit money, a seller should require a substantial deposit.

ARBITRATION
Another way to avoid protracted and expensive litigation is to include a clause that both seller and buyer will submit to bind-

ing arbitration if they cannot agree on the issues of the contract. Believe it or not, you really should have a lawyer word the clause to avoid hiring her later.

ATTORNEYS' FEES

If all else fails, you should have already agreed in advance who will pay the attorneys' fees in the event of litigation. In most cases you will not be awarded attorneys' fees unless provided for in the contract being litigated. The expense of litigation is sometimes enough to bring the other party to their senses, or to at least negotiate differences in good faith.

ACCEPTANCE TIME FRAME

A buyer's offer is valid until rescinded by the buyer. Let's say you missed this detail and did not hear back from the seller. You assumed the seller was not interested in your offer. You decided to purchase another business instead. Now, the seller of the first business decides he really does want to accept your offer. You either buy two businesses or risk the consequences! You can avoid this pitfall by putting a clause in the contract that states that the offer is only good for a specific period of time (three days, seven days, thirty days). After that period of time the offer is automatically re-

scinded. The time period could be considered to be too much pressure by some sellers but it often makes them take the time to consider your offer. My experience is that too short of a time period makes a seller believe you're being unreasonable and leaves little hope that she could work out all the details with you. If this is the way she feels, your offer might be rejected even though it would be considered a good offer otherwise.

CORPORATE ACKNOWLEDGMENT AND ACCEPTANCE

An agreement signed by a corporation can be disputed if it is not properly signed. To be sure, the seller should insist on a corporate resolution authorizing the corporation to enter into the contract. The resolution should show the authorized signatures as well. The corporate seal should be affixed. For a noncorporate entity or individual, a notarized document is the easiest to enforce. This subject should make you think about exactly who you are entering into contract with. Is it an individual? Is it a partnership? An LLC? A corporation, or some other entity? You are entitled as a seller to ask for information that will help you evaluate the financial strength of the entity making the offer. This information, which could include balance sheets or Dun & Bradstreet rating information, will usually not accompany an offer unless requested by the seller or the seller's professional.

Likewise, a prudent buyer who has significant financial strength might impress a seller if it is demonstrated with the offer. This could make a difference if more than one offer has been made.

PAYROLL TAXES AND OTHER LIABILITIES

The buyer must be satisfied that all payroll and related taxes have been paid before he settles on the business. Your attorney can check for you. The taxes you want to see satisfied are: withheld Federal taxes and unemployment insurance; withheld state and local amounts; and pension and other plans

DUE DILIGENCE TIME FRAME

If the contract has any contingencies, the seller should set a reasonable time for the contingencies to be investigated and/or satisfied. Failure to do so could cause your business to be unmarketable for an unreasonably long period of time. The way to control this is by specifying the time frame in the contract. You might state that any extensions of the time frame require mutual consent. Although any contract can be modified by mutual consent this statement shows clearly that your consent is required. For zoning or other issues, you may call the appropriate government entity and ask for a time estimate for the requirement. For license transfers, you also call the appropriate agency. It is always a good idea to look at the licenses and permits displayed in the place of business. You will learn the entity names licensed, as well as the government authorities you need to contact. Your professional and your lawyer can help you in this area. You may have a clause in the contract that causes the contingencies to become canceled or waived if the buyer does not notify you in writing that he is dissatisfied with any of the contingent matters. There should be a specific cut-off date for the buyer's notification(s).

TIME IS OF THE ESSENCE

Businesspeople either love or hate the term, "Time is of the essence." Basically, it means when a date or time is mentioned in the contract, there is no negotiating on the date or time. If the contract says March 13 then the matter needs to be resolved by March 13 — not the next day or next business day. This clause can make or break a transaction. It can force a buyer to perform or lose a sale for a seller. Courts looking at this term in a contract know exactly what it means. Be sure that you do.

What Do You Need to Learn More About?

If this book is a library copy, please do not write in it. Photocopy this page instead.

Circle the comfort level for each issue.	High			Low	
Deposit amount	5	4	3	2	1
Who holds deposit	5	4	3	2	1
Is deposit forfeitable	5	4	3	2	1
When will check be cashed	5	4	3	2	1
Increases in deposits	5	4	3	2	1
Terms of contract	5	4	3	2	1
Supplements:					
Personalty inventory	5	4	3	2	1
Accounts receivable list	5	4	3	2	1
Allocation of purchase price	5	4	3	2	1
Lease copy	5	4	3	2	1
Noncompete agreement	5	4	3	2	1
Copies of contracts & warranties	5	4	3	2	1
Supplier list	5	4	3	2	1
Customer lists	5	4	3	2	1
Resaleable merchandise	5	4	3	2	1
Obsolete merchandise	5	4	3	2	1
List of assets included	5	4	3	2	1
List of assets not included	5	4	3	2	1
Instructions to attorneys	5	4	3	2	1

Checklist continued on the next page

What Do You Need to Learn More About?

CHAPTER 8 COMFORT ZONE CHECKLIST

If this book is a library copy, please do not write in it. Photocopy this page instead.
Checklist continued from the previous page

Circle the comfort level for each issue.	High				Low
Prorations	5	4	3	2	1
Bills of sale	5	4	3	2	1
Lease terms and conditions	5	4	3	2	1
Transfer of licenses	5	4	3	2	1
Bulk sales requirement	5	4	3	2	1
Books and records	5	4	3	2	1
Seller's operation until settlement/transfer	5	4	3	2	1
Possession	5	4	3	2	1
Transition plan	5	4	3	2	1
Liabilities to be assumed	5	4	3	2	1
Sales and Use taxes	5	4	3	2	1
Liquidated damages	5	4	3	2	1
Arbitration	5	4	3	2	1
Attorneys' fees	5	4	3	2	1
Time frame for acceptance	5	4	3	2	1
Corporate acknowledgements	5	4	3	2	1
Payroll taxes and liabilities	5	4	3	2	1
Due diligence time frame	5	4	3	2	1
Time is of the essence	5	4	3	2	1

About your answers: There are no right or wrong answers. Study your responses to determine which items you need help with. Have your spouse or potential partner(s) fill in a copy of the checklist also. Discovering which subjects lack high comfort levels will help you choose professionals with the appropriate skills.

"Ponder the path of thy feet, and let all thy ways be established."

9

Choosing a Business Entity

- Sole Proprietorship
- Partnership
- Corporation
- Limited Liability Company (LLC)

Buyers should decide in advance what type of entity will own and/or operate the new business. Both your accountant and your lawyer should guide you through the process of selecting the right entity for you.

SOLE PROPRIETORSHIP
One person owns the business.

Financing
Based on your credit and net worth. With a new business don't be surprised if lenders are not confident about the potential cash

flow of the business. They likely will look for some secondary ability to repay any funds loaned.

No back up
If you are the sole proprietor you may have no other person to turn to in troubled times. Be careful not to extend yourself beyond your financial and physical capabilities.

Sole decision-making authority
You need not get others' consent to make business decisions. However, your lender might put some stringent controls on what you can do.

No need to share profits
While this sounds good right now, you should remember that you have no other person to share the losses with either.

No double taxation
Your profit or loss flows through to your personal tax return.

Help are paid wages
Fairly easy to hire and fire to improve business.

Personal liability for the business
You will be expected to pay all claims and damages arising out of the business. All withheld income and other taxes not paid will become direct liabilities against you. Liabilities not paid may attach to other personal assets.

PARTNERSHIP
Two or more persons or entities.

Double (or more) the workforce and management possible

Better backup for troubled times

More objectivity and ideas for decisions
(Two heads are better than one.)

More possible disputes
Control is diffused.

Better expansion capability

Risk is spread out
Assuming all partners put up capital and are financially liable, the risk may be lessened for each partner.

Share both the profit and the potential losses

Owners are customer-oriented
(usually more so than employees)

Better tax planning possible

In a partnership, it is possible to treat partners unequally for tax purposes. A properly structured partnership agreement can provide for one partner to have the depreciation tax advantage, another to receive income from loaned funds, and another to manage the business. This offers great flexibility if the planning is good (and in advance).

Help need not be paid

Partners can reach agreement where each has a different value – labor, ideas, capital. Control of the bottom line can be flexible (which may be crucial in the early stages of a newly acquired business).

Safety through buy/sell agreements

If something happens to one of the partners, it is possible to have an agreement that states who has the right to acquire his or her interest in the business. Life insurance can be purchased to provide the funding to purchase the interest from his or her estate.

Personal liability remains

Each partner could be responsible for the total amounts owed.

Caution

Partners don't always agree on issues. Equity is diluted. Each partner must have a dis-

street~smarts

Partnership Agreement

Don't form a partnership without a good partnership agreement. Items that must be covered by the agreement include type of business, amount of equity invested by each partner, division of profit and loss, partners' obligations and compensation, distribution of assets on dissolution or sale, duration of the partnership, dispute resolution or settlement procedures, restrictions of authority and expenditures, settlement in case of death or incapacitation, and provisions for changing the agreement when advisable or necessary.

tinct and substantial value to the business. Do not take partners unless you cannot operate the business by yourself.

CORPORATION

Many owners possible. If a corporation is formed as an S-Corporation (under IRS regulations), there is a limit on the number of shareholders and the corporation will not have double taxation as the income/loss passes through to the shareholders on their personal tax returns.

Limited liability
Lawsuits and/or judgments are brought against the corporation instead of the individual shareholders. This may allow the owners to avoid jeopardizing assets not involved in the business. (This does not mean that the individuals cannot be sued.)

Double taxation
Excepting the S-Corp mentioned above, the corporation generates its own tax liabilities.

Better for raising capital
Generally speaking, a corporation should make raising capital easier by offering flexibility. The corporation could issue stocks or bonds. It could guarantee loans with the shares of stock. This would give lenders the sense of gaining control if they felt it necessary. The strength of the business and its profitability will be key factors in this area.

Unequal ownership accomplished easily
Because the corporation has multiple shareholders, often with unequal investments in the business, unequal numbers of shares can be issued to gain the balance in equities.

Real world
Lenders to small corporations often require the shareholders to guarantee loans made to the corporation. This diminishes the benefit of having limited liability.

LIMITED LIABILITY COMPANY (LLC)
This entity is considered to be a corporation and is established under state statutes. Most states allow the formation of LLC's today but each state has different rules and regulations. The number of individuals in an LLC is also regulated. Check your state regulations.

No double taxation
Profit and loss flows through to shareholders (who are called "members").

Not accepted state to state
An LLC formed in one state must file as a "foreign corporation" in other states in which it intends to operate. Otherwise, mostly the same as a corporation.

GET GOOD COUNSEL
Talk with both your lawyer and your accountant before making the important decision of which business entity is right for your situation.

Which Entity Will You Choose?

Circle the comfort level for each issue.	High			Low	
Sole Proprietor	5	4	3	2	1
Partnership	5	4	3	2	1
Corporation	5	4	3	2	1
S-Corporation	5	4	3	2	1
Limited liability Corporation (LLC)	5	4	3	2	1

List advantages and disadvantages:

About your answers: There are no right or wrong answers. Study your responses to determine which items you need help with. Have your spouse or potential partner(s) fill in a copy of the checklist also. Discovering which subjects lack high comfort levels will help you choose professionals with the appropriate skills.

"Seest thou a man wise in his own conceit?
There is more hope of a fool than of him."

10

Dangers in Buying or Selling a Business

- Misleading Statements and/or Figures
- UCC Filings and Searches
- Books and Records
- Seller Ignorance
- Buyer Ignorance
- Licensing not Transferable
- Government Approvals
- Estoppels
- Undercapitalization
- Inexperience
- Undisclosed Partners or Owners
- Nontransferable Lease
- Nonconforming Use
- Business May Depend on Seller's Personality

Needless to say there are many dangers involved in buying or selling a business. This chapter includes fifteen for you to consider.

MISLEADING STATEMENTS AND / OR FIGURES

You will want to trust all information given to you, but you know you cannot. If you base your decision on wrong facts, it is likely you will make a bad decision. People don't have to lie to mislead you. They can repeat information they heard and believed. They can transmit facts and figures that were represented to them as true. They may be ignorant of the truth and just be offering their opinion. In my experience, this is the key area that causes problems for both buyers and sellers. If you need to transmit information to others in the buying/selling process, do so in writing. If possible, get the party to whom you transmitted the information to sign an acknowledgement that they received it. The very best way to keep communications clear is to have the recipient sign a copy of the document you transmitted.

UCC FILINGS AND SEARCHES

The danger is not checking to see if assets being purchased have liabilities to others on file. It is not possible to receive clear title to assets that are included in a Uniform Commercial Code filing without addressing the filing(s). Have your attorney check to be sure.

BOOKS AND RECORDS

Danger lives here. A good rule of thumb in most businesses is that deposits approximate disbursements. The money comes in and the money goes out. The question is: From where — to where? Sometimes it's just one person's opinion as to what column the entry should go in. *You* might have made a

different entry. Sometimes the entries are false. Sometimes no entry is made. Be careful in this area!

IGNORANCE ON THE PART OF THE SELLER

The seller did not know the health department requires an inspection of each restaurant at the time it changes hands or has a transfer of license. That's why she didn't tell you. I don't know why they didn't require a three-compartment sink for the previous operator. That will be $1,500 please.

IGNORANCE ON THE PART OF THE BUYER

We all thought it was so obvious that it did not need mentioning. How could you think this building had central air conditioning when it had an obvious window unit in operation? That will be $3,500 please.

ZONING LAWS

The zoning authorities are notorious for not having enough inspectors. They largely respond to complaints and then enforce compliance. The former operator never was cited for a complaint. He also never had the proper zoning. Please close your business until you get permission, if you can.

ESTOPPELS

The building I bought for my business has another tenant besides myself. They claim the landlord promised to replace the heating and air conditioning units. How can I be responsible just because I'm the new landlord? To eliminate this danger, you have each tenant execute, as a condition of the purchase contract, a paper called an *estoppel*. In this paper, which the landlord will have them sign, the tenants state what their current rent is, that they are not in default of any of the lease terms and conditions, and whether or not they have any claim against the current landlord. If there are problems with the tenants, you will find out before you own the real property.

LICENSING NOT TRANSFERABLE

I thought it was. Can I have my deposit back please?

UNDERCAPITALIZATION

I didn't think I would need this much money to get this business on track. Since business is slow, I can't get any additional financing.

GOVERNMENT APPROVALS

These may be costly, both in terms of money and time. And you have no guarantee approvals will be granted. They could require expensive changes (in the spirit of compromise) to receive the necessary approvals. This could involve sewer and water, fire protection, or dozens of other agencies.

INEXPERIENCE

The key employees quit. I don't know how to do what they did. I can't afford to hire and pay for a manager or someone with the proper experience. What do I do now?

UNDISCLOSED PARTNERS OR OWNERS

A title search is usually not possible for a small business. You can look on each license and know who some of the owners are, but you could miss one. Even if the seller promises he is the only one, how can you know for sure? For anything other than a sole proprietorship (more than one name on licenses) you can ask for documentation of ownership, such as a partnership agreement or list of shareholders.

NONTRANSFERABLE LEASE

This needs to be resolved before you take over the business. Transfer and/or assignment is not automatic. The landlord may require an increase in rent to agree to your assignment. He may tighten up on terms and conditions. He may try to take control over you — control that he did not have under the old lease. By the way, if you are negotiating for a new lease or an assignment, this is a good time to talk with the landlord about extending the lease or getting more favorable terms and conditions.

NONCONFORMING USE

You've heard the term *grandfathered*. This means that the new codes would not permit the business to be in this location in today's political climate. Businesses can lose their

nonconforming status in various ways. If the building suffers major damage you may not be able to rebuild. If the business fails to operate for a specific period of time you can lose the status. It is always wise to check with the local (and county and state) authorities.

BUSINESS MAY DEPEND ON SELLER'S PERSONALITY

Just because someone else is successful at a business does not mean you will be. If your business depends on a limited number of customers or clients, you may wish to interview them (with the seller's permission) prior to taking over the business. This would be a good time to ask them how the business might be improved. Could you add products and/or services that would increase your sales and make customers happier?

Timing Is Everything!

Don't be in too much of a hurry — but don't wait too long. Remember that all sellers and buyers are people. Be observant to determine what their situations are and find ways to make the situations work for you. Be especially aware of your own limitations. You may have to walk away from a sale or purchase to make it work. Sometimes a break in the flow of a purchase or sale will help — or hurt. Consider timing as part of the negotiation process. In a seasonal business you should negotiate in the slower months and take title just before the higher months. A seller with a health problem will need a quick sale. Sometimes speed will mean more than the highest price. Some buyers and sellers have a fear of speed in a transaction. You may have to slow down to accommodate the personalities in the transaction.

Do You Understand the Dangers of Each?

CHAPTER 10 COMFORT ZONE CHECKLIST

If this book is a library copy, please do not write in it. Photocopy this page instead.

Circle the comfort level for each issue.	High				Low
Misleading statements and/or figures	5	4	3	2	1
UCC filings and searches	5	4	3	2	1
Ignorance on the seller's part	5	4	3	2	1
Ignorance on the buyer's part	5	4	3	2	1
Zoning laws	5	4	3	2	1
Licensing nontransferable	5	4	3	2	1
Governmental approvals	5	4	3	2	1
Estoppels	5	4	3	2	1
Undercapitalization	5	4	3	2	1
Inexperience	5	4	3	2	1
Undisclosed partners or owners	5	4	3	2	1
Nontransferable lease	5	4	3	2	1
Nonconforming uses	5	4	3	2	1
Effect of seller's personality on business	5	4	3	2	1
Timing	5	4	3	2	1

About your answers: There are no right or wrong answers. Study your responses to determine which items you need help with. Have your spouse or potential partner(s) fill in a copy of the checklist also. Discovering which subjects lack high comfort levels will help you choose professionals with the appropriate skills.

"Take counsel, execute judgment."

11

The Real Property— Lease or Buy?

- Lease Rates and Terms
- Tomorrow's Rates and Terms
- Length of Lease for Recovery of Investment
- Portability of Business
- Control of Future Events
- Landlords Are People Too
- Affordability
- Balance Sheet vs. Profit and Loss Functions
- Separate Investment
- Reversibility
- Enhancement at Time of Sale

Of course, it is not always possible to purchase the real estate along with the business. I don't mean from the seller — that's always negotiable. But if the business is in a building with other users, you may not be able or willing to purchase it. Depending on your business plan, it may not be wise to purchase until you season the new business. I will limit my discussion here to the cases in which you have the opportunity to purchase and explain how to evaluate the alternatives.

LEASE RATES AND TERMS

A crucial component of the decision whether to lease or buy will be the lease rates and terms. In some older buildings the owner's basis is very low. He can charge low lease rates and still realize a good investment return on the property. Some owners feel the best way to reduce turnover of tenants and maintain high occupancy is to keep the rental rates low. If it would cost much more to purchase (dollars per month) it may be wise to lease instead. Most leases today are *triple-net leases* (NNN). This means the owner receives the base rents plus an amount to reimburse him for your pro rata share of real estate taxes, insurance, and any maintenance of the grounds or common area. When you add all the charges together you have the total amount you must pay monthly for rents. The reasoning behind the NNN lease is that it allows the owner to receive income that is not variable or eaten up by rising costs and inflation. Sometimes these charges are referred to in a lease as *additional rents*. This is a legal term that makes delinquent charges easier to collect in court. If an owner does not ask for these additional charges, the rent is called *gross rents*. Of course there are many variations — an owner can structure rentals in any way he wishes. Your job is to understand the charges and negotiate what you must pay.

Another factor is the terms. How long (or how short) will the lease be? If you feel you can grow the business you are buying and that you may have to expand in a year or two, you may want a relatively short lease term. Since you may have to relocate the business, you don't want to have the obligation and liability of a lease beyond the timetable you anticipate. If you are not sure how the business will grow, you may ask for a short lease term and perhaps an option(s) to renew the lease for an additional period(s). Since this does not cost the owner anything, he often will grant requests for options. The option means you may stay or leave at the end of each term. You are not obligated, but the owner is.

There are other terms in a lease that will be favorable or unfavorable to you. Leases may have noncompete clauses that specify certain uses/sales you may not engage in. These clauses may seriously affect the flexibility of your business. The intent of the noncompete clause is to protect other tenants at the property and eliminate competition among them. You would be wise to ask for such clauses to be placed in future leases in a multi-tenant property. Since each owner usually has a lease form they prefer, ask to see a blank copy well in advance of negotiating final rents and terms.

TOMORROW'S RATES AND TERMS

When you purchase a property, the monthly costs do not rise dramatically. The hazard insurance and real estate taxes may rise but assuming you are smart enough to get a fixed rate, the mortgage payment will remain level. When you lease it's a different story. Owners want to see the income increase over time. They will either negotiate a *graduated rents schedule* in which the future rents are set out in a table, or require Consumer Price Index (CPI) increases annually. The intent of adjusting rents annually to reflect increases in the CPI is to bring rents up so they are paid in real dollars. The use of CPI increases should not affect your business much, since you probably will be charging inflated prices for your goods and services. However, the owner's basic cost of mortgage payments does not rise. He makes out very well — so you can negotiate. Watch out for minimum increases. Here the owner will say something like, "Rents to be adjusted annually to reflect increases in the CPI but in no event less than five percent increase annually." You don't want to be paying increased rents during periods of low inflation or recession. If this clause must be in the lease, ask for a ceiling on increases. Your phrase might add, "but in no event more than eight percent increase annually." What's good for the goose is good for the gander.

LENGTH OF LEASE FOR RECOVERY OF INVESTMENT

Most asset financing is offered over five to seven years. If you are obligated to make payments over a set number of years, then you should be able to stay in the business location at least that long. Explaining this to a reasonable owner will usually be sufficient to get the lease term long enough to suit your needs.

PORTABILITY OF BUSINESS

One of the worst disasters in the business world is outgrowing the location. If you can double the business, but patrons have no place to park, you are in trouble. If you can add product lines but have no shelf space left you are in trouble. You must consider these possibilities in advance, and include them in your business plan. Project the most favorable scenario of business growth and find out if the property will facilitate the potential growth. This will guide your selection of the lease's term. In a multi-tenant property you may ask for the "first right of refusal on adjoining space." This means every time a space next to you becomes vacant or available, you have the right to lease that space also. Be careful to mention how the rents will be determined in such a situation. Usually you can get an owner to agree to "the average rents in the market area" but the question then becomes how the average is determined. It might be possible to have an owner agree to rents "equal to the square footage rents being paid at the original space." Granting you the "first right of refusal" does not cost an owner anything. He should allow this clause as it will turn a future problem into a success for him.

CONTROL OF FUTURE EVENTS

Purchasing the property gives you control of the future and more flexibility than leasing. Even if you relocate the business to larger or better-located space, you still have control and flexibility. You have control over the monthly costs, the ability to change the physical structure without permission, and expanded decision making in many other areas. In a multi-tenant property, you may change the tenant mix to alter the nature of the product or service mix to the community. When you lease, you need permission from a decision maker who has a different vision than you do. Increased control can be increased profitability. You don't have to increase your business's rent unless it is advantageous to do so, perhaps to manipulate (within reason) your taxable income.

LANDLORDS ARE PEOPLE TOO

The decision to lease or purchase is greatly affected by the lease rates and terms. Remember to show respect to the owner before you begin negotiating. One way to do this is to meet informally with the owner to determine his goals for the property. If you can assure the owner that you and your business will be good for the property, you may negotiate more favorable rates and terms. The owner's goal should be to maintain full or high occupancy while minimizing the risks of owning the property. There may be other issues such as pride of ownership, passive management, or power. Take the time to treat your new landlord as a person. Many tenants do not.

AFFORDABILITY

It may cost more to buy a property than to lease it. This is relatively simple to calculate. Talk with your lender to determine the monthly cost of a mortgage and how much cash they will require as a down payment. Include consideration of the financing of the business and/or business assets at the same time. Anticipate the lease costs (you may still be negotiating) and compare.

You may find that a better use of your available capital or borrowing power is to purchase equipment and/or inventory. If you can be sure of a better return on your capital by using it in the business, you might decide it is better to lease. Of course you will never realize appreciation by leasing. And in a multi-tenant property the other tenants will not be helping you pay off the mortgage unless you purchase. Calculate and determine what you can afford, and then consider the best uses of your capital and/or borrowing power.

BALANCE SHEET VS. PROFIT AND LOSS FUNCTIONS

A healthy business will not only have a good profit and loss statement (income statement) but also a good balance sheet (statement of net worth). If you are not comfortable with accounting and taxation, you should seek help from your accountant. A business owner who purchases the property will show the value of the asset on the balance sheet along with the liability and resultant equity. The equity may serve as collateral to a lender to secure debt. A lease will not show on the balance sheet, except perhaps as a footnote. If you are heavily leveraged, you may not want more borrowings on your balance sheet. This would be a good reason to lease instead. The profit and loss statement will show the cash flow available to a business owner either to live on or to make loan payments, or both. Both the balance sheet and the income statement are important indications of the financial health of an individual or business.

Be aware that not all financial statements are the same. If an accountant declares the statements to be *audited*, he needs to verify all information to be sure it is correct. This is expensive. Small businesses often ask for *unaudited statements*. These are usually marked by the accountant (in a cover letter) with something similar to "these statements are prepared from books and records furnished by the client." Obviously, you should depend less on the latter statements.

You may find it wise to purchase the business property personally and then to lease it to your business. Tax advantages are possible. Income from a rental property is *passive income*. Income from the business is *active income*. They are taxed differently. By leasing the property to your business, you may adjust the rental rate to increase or decrease either passive or active income. Of course, more income to the owner of the property means less income to the business which is leasing, and vice versa. The IRS regulations require that the rents be normal for the market area but this still leaves a great deal of flexibility. If your business will be a corporation, or if you form a corporation to be the owner of the property, there is still added flexibility. Discuss these matters with your accountant or tax attorney.

SEPARATE INVESTMENT

When making your decision whether to lease or buy the business property, treat the property as a separate investment. Try to consider the purchase of the property as if you were not purchasing the business. If the business fails or outgrows the property, that is exactly what you will have — a separate investment. If you would not want to be stuck with the property later, then don't buy it now.

REVERSIBILITY

It is always wise in a business plan to anticipate what you can do if everything goes wrong, or if substantial changes occur. If you need to dispose of the business for any reason, you can sell the business and rent out the property to the new business owner. You can lease both the business and the property. You can sell the business and the property together. But these options are only available if you own the business property.

What can you do if you are renting and need to get out of the lease? You may offer to buy yourself out by offering a sum of money to the landlord. You might offer to continue making rent payments until the landlord secures another tenant. Be sure you require him to be diligent in locating a new tenant if you offer this. Perhaps a better exit strategy would be to find the replacement tenant yourself. If you do a good job you may be able to sublease (usually with the landlord's permission), charge

more than you are paying, and keep the difference. Caution: you may not want to be landlord in a building you don't own. More than likely, you will still be primarily liable for the rent payments. You may find yourself responsible for the behavior and actions of the subtenant.

ENHANCEMENT AT TIME OF SALE

Whether you lease from yourself or others, good terms are crucial to getting a better price when you decide to sell your business. More favorable rates and terms will reflect in more favorable monthly costs to a buyer. This generally will allow the buyer to pay a higher price for the business. If you negotiate the most favorable rates and terms when you enter into a lease, then the job is done. But if you buy the property, you have the ability to change or enhance the rates and terms to a buyer when the time comes to sell your business. You can give the buyer a low rate of rent for the first year or two. This will help guarantee the success of the business and a more secure tenant.

street~smarts

Purchase Whenever Possible

That's what I would do assuming the price and terms were right. You'll have more control, more flexibility, better reversibility, and better tax treatment. You'll have possible appreciation of the property, principal paydown on the mortgage — and, best of all, no landlord for a partner.

Will You Lease or Buy — and Why?

If this book is a library copy, please do not write in it. Photocopy this page instead.

Circle the comfort level for each issue.	High				Low
Lease rates & terms	5	4	3	2	1
Tomorrow's rates & terms	5	4	3	2	1
Length of lease/recovery of investment	5	4	3	2	1
Portability of business	5	4	3	2	1
Control of future events	5	4	3	2	1
"Landlords are people, too"	5	4	3	2	1
Affordability of real property	5	4	3	2	1
Balance sheet vs. profit and loss functions	5	4	3	2	1
Separate investment concept	5	4	3	2	1
Reversibility	5	4	3	2	1
Enhancement at time of sale	5	4	3	2	1

About your answers: There are no right or wrong answers. Study your responses to determine which items you need help with. Have your spouse or potential partner(s) fill in a copy of the checklist also. Discovering which subjects lack high comfort levels will help you choose professionals with the appropriate skills.

"A false balance is not good."

12

Valuation of a Small Business

- Income Approach
- Market Comparison
- Replacement Cost
- Real Value

"A Chart! A Chart! My Kingdom for a Chart!" I can communicate this information well with a flip chart and some markers, but not so easily with this seminar-in-a-book. Not that I have all the answers to the subject matter — but there are some rules of thumb and common sense approaches to determining value. Some involve knowledge of accounting, building costs and other matters. As you follow the approaches in this chapter, try to make some of the calculations with some made-up assumptions. Get a pencil and paper and let's work through this chapter together.

INCOME APPROACH

This method of valuation makes conclusions based on the ability of the business to generate income.

Using the NOI

What you want to know about a business is the net operating income (NOI). Unfortunately this term is not clearly understood by many. NOI is the total income from all sources minus all the expenses to generate the income. In a sales business you would subtract the cost of the goods sold and all the expenses incurred to make the sales. You do not subtract mortgage payments. A buyer might purchase for cash and not have any mortgage payments. Do not subtract depreciation, interest expense, or amortization. These are tax preference items and do not belong in the real world income calculation.

If you are a small business that does not pay a salary to the business owner but takes the profit or loss as compensation, do not subtract any draws or other compensation. The NOI will be your compensation. If you are buying a business that requires management other than yourself, it is appropriate to include the management costs as an expense. It can be part of the payroll expense or shown separately.

Once you have calculated the NOI of the business, multiply it by 1.0 and also multiply it by 3.0. For most small businesses this establishes a full range of potential market values (prices). Let's use the example of a business with an NOI of $100,000. The range of prices should be from $100,000-$300,000. Looking at this range objectively, it appears that you could work for free for one to three years and the business would have paid itself off. Prices established with this method generally do not include inventory. Inventory is additional and is purchased at cost or market, whichever is lower. In the real world, businesses are not always in this price range. This is only a rule of thumb. But the idea of determining the value based on the amount of income that can be generated makes a great deal of sense. You are really buying a potential income stream. If you find that the business you are considering does not fall in this range then ask how the sales price was determined. Ask the seller to justify the price.

Example #1

The business nets $45,000 per year (NOI)
Times 1: $45,000 (Low end of range)
Times 3: $135,000 (High end of range)

Example #2

Business nets $123,000 per year (NOI)
Times 1: $123,000 (Low end of range)
Times 2: $369,000 (High end of range)

Note

> Calculations using this method are based on the net operating income (NOI), and do not include amounts for the financing costs of the business for a purchaser. They do not consider any income tax liabilities. They do not include the purchase of any real estate that may be associated with the business, but will include an expense item for rents in the calculation of income.

Businesses that have specialized equipment, strong name recognition, patents, or other special values will not use this method of setting a sales price. Each of these components will have their own value in the sales price. Add all the values together and see if the price is fair. On the other hand, you may find that by using this method this business has no value at all. You may still buy the platform at some price you are willing to pay. The cost could be much less than starting the business by yourself. Or you may buy uniqueness. Consider the prices being fetched by the owners of desirable URLs by the new dot.coms!

Using the cap rate

Another way to determine value is to use a *capitalization rate* (cap rate). Here I could really use the flip chart. Using this method you can calculate the return that an ex-penditure will bring you — dependent upon the income it generates. Let me give you the formula:

$$\text{Income (NOI)} / \text{Price (Value)}$$
$$= \text{capitalization rate (percent return)}$$

I hope you remember your algebra. If you have two of the ingredients you can calculate the third. Let's use an example: An asset valued at $100,000 produces an income of $10,000. The cap rate is 10%.
Calculate it yourself:

$$\$10,000/\$100,000 = .10 \ (10\%)$$

If you invest $100,000 and want a 10% return you must get an income of $10,000. If an asset has an income of $10,000 and you want a 10% return you can spend $100,000 to purchase the asset (or the income stream). This approach is especially good for buildings. You must be careful not to use this approach for the value of the business since there is an extra ingredient. You must operate and manage the business. Your time and talent are not included in the cap rate calculation. But you certainly can evaluate the real property component of a purchase using the cap rate calculation.

The return you desire will dictate the amount of money you can spend for the asset or business. Examine the following calculations — all for the same business and see what your conclusions are:

NOI = $40,000 per year
How much should you spend?

Cap Rate	Value/Price
8%	$500,000
9%	$444,444
10%	$400,000
11%	$363,636
12%	$333,333
15%	$266,667

This method is especially effective for purchasing income-producing real estate rather than business opportunities. You will find the cap rate especially useful to determine the value of the real estate component of a business purchase, but you can use it for any income stream from any asset. How much will your business be willing to pay as rents for the use of the property? Assuming your business will pay the real estate taxes, insurance, and all the other expenses of maintaining the property, this will be your NOI as an owner/investor of the property.

Cash on cash return (COC)

This final method, cash on cash return, which involves using the income to determine value, is a real-life exercise in numbers. Here you will be working with not only the NOI but also all the costs of the purchase, including the interest costs and even the principal paydown on a mortgage, if any. The formula is:

NOI - ADS (annual debt service)
= Cash Flow (before taxes)
Cash Flow / Investment Base
(actual cash down)
= COC return

[Please refer to the table of examples on the next page for the following discussion.]

What happened in Example #2? There was not enough money to make all the payments. There are two ways you can cure a potential negative cash flow on any purchase. The first would be to increase the down payment cash. This would make the payments lower to accommodate the cash flow. The negative cash flow would turn into a positive cash flow. Another method to solve the problem would be to calculate the amount of money expected to pay the negative cash flow over the entire period you expect negative cash flow. In a business you expect to "grow" this could be a year or two. Chart the expected negative cash flow, add all the monthly amounts together and set aside an equal amount in an account from which you can make the payments when needed. Because you did not use the cash to increase the down payment you will still have access to this account in an emergency.

Comparisons of Cap Rate Results with COC

The following examples compare the results of the cap rate with COC

Example #1

Business/Commercial property is priced at $350,000

NOI	=	$42,000
Cap Rate	=	12%
Down Payment of 25%	=	$87,500 (Investment Base)
Mortgage of 75%	=	$237,500
ADS (9.5% int over 20 yrs)	=	$26,566/yr ($2213.81 x 12)
NOI	=	$42,000
ADS	=	-$26,566
Cash Flow (Before tax)	=	$15,434
Cash on Cash Return	=	17.639%
		($15,434 divided by $87,500)

Example #2

Business/Commercial property is priced at $450,000

NOI	=	$36,000
Cap Rate	=	8%
Down Payment of 25%	=	$112,500 (Investment Base)
Mortgage of 75%	=	$337,500
ADS (9.5% int over 20 yrs)	=	$37,751/yr ($3145.94 x 12)
NOI	=	$36,000
ADS	=	-$37,751
Cash Flow (Before tax)	=	-$1,751
Cash on Cash Return	=	negative
		($112,500 divided by -$1,751)

Dr. Tuttle's Magic Zero

How would you like to compare the corner store value to the value of the Empire State Building — without a calculator? Then use Dr. Tuttle's Magic Zero! Here's how it works. Calculate the net operating income for the property (business/asset/etc.) for one year. Add a zero. That's an approximate value!

Why does it work? The question is: How much would you be willing to spend to purchase an asset that will bring you $10,000 per year, if you expected a 10% return on that asset? (The $10,000 is the NOI.) The answer is $100,000. You spend the $100,000 and get a return of $10,000 per year. That is a 10% return.

Simple? The only adjustment you might make to this formula is if you want a greater return than the 10% used in the Magic Zero formula. Plug the new return rate into the formula above, and you will be able to easily calculate how much you can afford to spend for any income stream.

Other Methods

There are other multipliers and value calculations that can be used. Your accountant will understand these methods and can help if needed.

- Cash on Cash — After Tax (COC/AT)
- Equity Rate of Return (ERR)
- Internal Rate of Return (IRR)
- Financial Management Rate of Return (FMRR)

When buying a business it is unlikely that you will employ all of these methods but using them is a good way to compare alternative opportunities to see which you would like to investigate further. Again — it is not all about numbers.

MARKET COMPARISON

Even if an abundance of good data were available that compared sales prices of other similar businesses (there usually is not), there would be a weakness to the market comparison approach. No two businesses are really the same. And reporting of sales prices for businesses purchased is not a science. The reporting is either voluntary or is in expectation of taxation or tax consequences. Therefore, prices are often manipulated. There are some databases available (business brokers sometimes use them) but I feel this is the least trustworthy approach to value of all those available. As with any market comparison, values of comparable businesses would have to be weighted or adjusted because of their differences. Who would you trust to make the adjustments? If such data is available, you can use the information to aid in your decision making — just do not place too much emphasis on the values. There is software listed in the appendix for those with statistical brains. Using this software (which can cost several hundred dollars), you can view similar businesses sold together with expressions of the sales price in relationship to sales, income, and other useful correlations. Remember — this is all theory. The questions are how much will the seller take, and how much will the buyer be willing to pay?

REPLACEMENT COST

This method calculates the value of all the assets as if you needed to pay to replace them. Accountants often depreciate the values of assets to adjust for their age or condition. Let's look at some of the components you are likely to find in a business.

Equipment

One assumption used when buying a business is that all of the equipment necessary to operate the business is in good repair. Often this is not true. Your contract should specify that each piece of equipment is in good working order and you should check each piece before purchasing the business. You can use today's cost of the equipment for your calculations but the life of the equipment generally will be shortened because it is used. You might ask to see maintenance records and/or current contracts for maintenance. Then you must make a judgment as to value. It is not wise to take the seller's word for value. His book value might be nice since he has depreciated the equipment since it was placed into use.

Inventory

As discussed earlier you should pay the seller's actual cost or the market value, whichever is lower. You should weed out items that are not readily saleable or that are obsolete or damaged. Some buyers hire an independent appraiser to place a value on the inventory. Some ask the suppliers of the products in inventory to make the calculation for them. In the end you want to be able to make a profit on the inventory when you sell it so you don't want to pay too much.

The value for inventory replacement will be the current cost to purchase items needed for the business. In an inflationary market, you might actually pay more than a seller paid previously. In a recessionary market, inventory might cost you less.

New lease

Sometimes the assumption of a lease can be done at very favorable rates. If the lease rate is well below market, it has a distinct value. Its value would be the difference between the actual rate and the market rate. Your professional should be able to help you with the knowledge necessary to ascertain this value.

Down time

Small businesses often operate without a profit for the first two or three years. Buying an existing business that is showing a positive cash flow saves you the money you would have spent operating without profit. I call this *down time*. Most sellers would not think of charging for this value separately, but it is somewhere in the price. You need to decide if it is a real value to you in calculating what price you will offer to buy the business.

Leasehold improvements

One of the positive aspects of buying an existing business is that it is all set up and ready to operate. It probably wasn't that way when the business started. Someone had to build the counters, shelving, and storage closets, install carpeting, suspend the ceilings, put in restrooms, and make the improvements to the empty space. You would have to pay for this if you re-

street~smarts

I have one final word about value. If there is any distress in the business — cancel all the considerations in this chapter! Time pressure. Negative cash flow. Suppliers requiring COD. Personal problems. Unusual hours of operation. Sales or profit showing decline. Absentee management in situations where the owner should be managing. These are all signs of distress. When a seller is under pressure he will make decisions and act in ways you cannot anticipate or understand. Negotiate.

placed the business. Calculate the value to your business. If the improvements belong to a landlord, they still have value but should not be included in calculating a price for the business. You are not buying them — they are being charged for in the rents.

The absolute highest price you should be willing to pay for a business is what it would cost you to set up across the street and build the business. Of course you would have competition if you did that. No matter where you put your new business you would have the existing competition. It's a good exercise to value the items I've discussed here and construct the highest price you should pay. Then negotiate for the existing business.

REAL VALUE

The real value of the business is set in the marketplace. It is the price a willing buyer would pay that a willing seller would accept. That's the price you are going to pay.

I offer some final cautions. Risk is not considered in any of these methods or calculations. In fact, risk is almost impossible to measure or calculate. Your risk tolerance is something only you can define. I tell my clients that a sound investment is one that will allow you to sleep at night. If you are uncomfortable with any purchase, slow down and determine why. If you cannot handle the risk — move on to some other opportunity.

All of these methods or calculations in this chapter involve assumptions. Even a well-documented cash flow can change. Things can get better or worse. Costs can change. Income can change. Therefore, returns can change and values will change. A wise purchaser will forecast future economic conditions, costs of financing, and conditions of the type of business as well.

street~smarts

A Word of Caution

When valuations are required for divorce proceedings or estate purposes, hire an independent professional. Make sure the person you hire knows the exact purpose — it will affect his judgment!

Do You Know These Valuation Techniques?

CHAPTER 12 COMFORT ZONE CHECKLIST

If this book is a library copy, please do not write in it. Photocopy this page instead.

Circle the comfort level for each technique.	High			Low	
Income approach	5	4	3	2	1
Net Operating Income (NOI)	5	4	3	2	1
Capitalization rate (cap rate)	5	4	3	2	1
Cash-on-cash return	5	4	3	2	1
Market comparison method	5	4	3	2	1
Replacement cost method	5	4	3	2	1
The Magic Zero formula	5	4	3	2	1

About your answers: There are no right or wrong answers. Study your responses to determine which items you need help with. Have your spouse or potential partner(s) fill in a copy of the checklist also. Discovering which subjects lack high comfort levels will help you choose professionals with the appropriate skills.

"For what shall it profit a man, if he shall gain the whole world,
and lose his own soul?"

13

Financing— Where to Get It

- Savings
- Cash Value of Life Insurance
- Relatives
- Equity Mortgages
- Lines of Credit
- Equity Partners
- Investors
- Banks
- SBA Guaranteed Loans
- SBICs
- Mortgage Brokers
- Venture Capital Groups
- Stock Market
- Plastic
- Business Plastic
- Seller Financing

In your business plan you must determine how much capital you will need to purchase and operate the business. This can vary greatly in different business scenarios, even for similar business opportunities. Whether you lease or buy can make a significant difference. How much will you have to pay for the business? How much will the business require in the way of new equipment, advertising, anticipated changes, and adequate working capital to get you up and started?

Be aware that there are two basic types of loans — short-term and long-term. A short-term loan is considered one that has a maturity of up to one year. You might need one of these loans for working capital, accounts receivable financing, and/or a line of credit for operations. Long-term loans are greater than one year to maturity and can be as long as twenty to thirty years. Long-term loans are used for major business expenses such as purchasing real estate and facilities, construction, durable equipment, furniture and fixtures, and similar uses. Vehicles and equipment are usually financed with maturities between five and seven years, although some financing packages will grant longer terms for repayment. When looking for financing, there are a number of options to explore.

SAVINGS

If you have the money in the bank that's a good place to start. Avoid excessive borrowing. Adding the interest costs could hurt your new venture. Consider retirement accounts that will allow you early withdrawal. Although you may pay a penalty, it may still be cost effective.

CASH VALUE OF LIFE INSURANCE

You shouldn't have any cash value in your life insurance in any event. Buy term insurance in an amount equal to or greater than your present coverage and then cash out — cancel — the whole life policy. Instead of letting the insurance company invest your excess premiums, invest them yourself. Why should you borrow your own money from them? And then pay interest? But use caution: Never cancel the old policies until you have the new one(s) in your possession. You don't want to be without life insurance for your family.

RELATIVES

You might find a relative who will wish you well and then put his money where his mouth is. Ask. You might offer a preferred return (you make payments to them before you take any profit out), a portion of the profits, or, as a last resort, a partnership in the equity in the business.

EQUITY MORTGAGES

Consider a first, second, or third mortgage on real estate you own for the financing. I know what you're going to say. "I don't want to put my house up as collateral!" Where do you think you can find a lender that won't require your house as collateral? And if your business does poorly or fails, how do you think you are going to satisfy outstanding obligations? You are going to sell your house.

LINES OF CREDIT

Besides the home equity lines of credit, banks offer commercial lines of credit — not easily, and not to everyone. If you can demonstrate prior experience in the business you are about to acquire and have sound credit, you may find a lender to give you a line of credit. The interest rate will be higher than a mortgage on your home. It just is. Lines of credit can be secured by inventory, receivables, equipment, or anything that is readily convertible into cash. Yes, they will also ask you to pledge your home for a new business venture.

EQUITY PARTNERS

Instead of borrowing money you may find a partner who will put his money up for a piece of the business. This is not a working partner. She will not come to the shop and work. She might expect payments in addition to a portion of the profits. She may demand to have input on all major decisions made in the business. More than likely she will also expect a preferred return. When the business sells, she will be entitled to a share of the profits upon sale. If the interest costs are not a factor, and you cannot get reasonable financing from another source, you might consider this option.

INVESTORS

Investors are people who will loan you money for the return of principal and interest. You could offer a piece of the profits but not have to offer any equity or ownership. Sometimes called an *angel* or *sugardaddy*, these people are hard to find. Some investors are reasonable. Some like to come into the place and feel involved. The prettier your business appears to them the more likely they are to invest. Racing cars? Fancy restaurant? Box seats at major ballgames? These attract investors. As opposed to equity partners, these investors do not own any part of your business. This is called *debt financing* (as opposed to *equity financing*).

BANKS

Many banks operate profitable commercial lending departments. They are interested in helping businesses and also establishing deposit relationships with business people. However, when it comes to buying a business, a loan from a commercial bank may not be easy to obtain.

Let's start with the basic elements they need to consider your loan. They look for "the 4 C's": Character, Credit, Collateral, and Cash Flow.

Character. Start by demonstrating your character. Include a personal and business profile with the submission of any loan request. Meet personally with the loan officer so he may get a good feeling about you. Dress well. Be prepared to answer his business and personal questions.

Credit. Obtain a copy of your credit report ahead of time. If any negative items appear, take action to remedy them. If you don't have much established credit, include a list of financial references in your loan package. This might include a landlord to whom you pay rent, the utility company, trade suppliers, and anyone who has trusted you but does not report to the credit agencies.

Collateral. There must be something that can be sold to satisfy the debt if you fail to pay. This can include both personal and business assets. If collateral is not available in the full amount of the loan, you will need to demonstrate a secondary source of income to repay the loan. Life insurance in the amount of the loan may be required.

Cash Flow. Lenders need to know that money will be available to make loan payments. They will calculate a debt-coverage ration (DCR). You will need to show a greater cash flow than the required payments. It is not unusual for a bank to desire 125-140% of the monthly payments in cash flow. Income from other sources may be considered if the source is reliable, and available for the full term of the loan.

If you can offer all "4 C's", you may be

a candidate for a bank loan. Rates vary among banks, and can change quickly with changes in the economy. A bank may only lend with a variable rate of interest - this lessens the risk of the bank's profitability with changes in the economy. Ask about rates, terms, and conditions early in the process. Ask the banker what types of loan programs they offer.

Any lender will be looking for experience in the type of business for which financing is requested. If you don't have direct experience in the field, be prepared to demonstrate why you believe you will be successful in the venture.

You should have at least one banker on your professional team. Even if you don't use a bank for the acquisition of a business you will need banking services while operating it. More information about banks and banking will be found in the next chapter.

SBA GUARANTEED LOANS

The Small Business Administration (SBA) no longer makes loans to small businesses. They haven't done so for years. What they do is guarantee a portion of the loan to the lender — to make the loan safer. This makes the lender more willing to make the loan. Should you go to a bank to apply for an SBA guaranteed loan? Not all banks process this type of loan. Ask before you submit.

There are a variety of SBA *preferred lenders* you can work with; not all are banks. The firms given this title can process all the paperwork and the SBA will then make the approval. There are some rules and expectations. They want to know you will have employees. Providing jobs is one of their hot buttons. The prospects for getting a small loan (less than $250,000) are actually much less than for getting a larger loan. One of the ways to increase the loan request is to purchase the property that houses the business — that will get their attention. The maximum loan at the time of this writing is $1,000,000, but it is expected to be increased soon. And there are ways to get more. You can apply for funding for all parts of the business — the real estate, the equipment, the leasehold improvements, and even working capital. The loan-to-value can be up to 85%, and the amortization periods can be as long as twenty to twenty-five years. The longer period of amortization will make the payments lower. The interest rate might be much lower than a regular bank loan. It is possible to secure an 80/10/10 loan. The lender provides 80% of the need, the seller carries a note for 10%, and you come up with just 10% in cash. Ask about this one!

There is a regional SBA office somewhere near you. Look them up and give them a call. Ask your professional for a list of good preferred lenders in your area.

SBICs

If you are going to purchase a sizable business and have some sophistication you might want to inquire into a Small Business Investment Corporation (SBIC). These corporations target businesses that have significant expansion possibilities. Instead of the traditional debt position (borrowing), the SBIC will require equity in the business venture. They will place controls on the enterprise and most likely will want to sit on the board of directors of your company. They bring experience and knowledge to the table but dilute ownership. Before considering funding from an SBIC you will need to do a good deal of reading to understand what they really do. Try all the other ways first.

MORTGAGE BROKERS

When purchasing the real estate you might want to contact a mortgage broker. Mortgage brokers take your package and shop for the best rates and terms for all the banks they do business with. They often provide value by getting cost-effective financing. Ask about the fees and points before you submit all the information. Do not pay any fees in advance. By the way — get good personal references for the broker you intend to transact with. Not everyone who calls themselves a mortgage broker is what they claim. Always know who you are dealing with.

VENTURE CAPITAL GROUPS

Venture capital groups also require you to have a sizable business and a great need for capital. They are also looking for substantially sophisticated business ventures. Venture capital groups are created to help young businesses get started and grow. They often require equity in the company and sometimes require membership on your board of directors. They will have you agree to decision-making controls. Get legal and financial counsel before entering into any agreement with a venture capital group.

STOCK MARKET

Grow the business. Go public. Retire rich. Those with success stories like this are few and far between. Notice, you have to control the business first, so this is not a good source of financing for acquiring a business unless you are expanding by acquisition. If someone wants you to purchase a corporate shell for a hundred thousand or more and take you public, run — don't walk — to the exit, and get help!

PLASTIC

Some people finance with business cards. *Don't do it.* The interest rates are too high. If you can't qualify for conventional financing, fix the problem or buy something you

> If you're smarter than me and insist on financing your business venture or purchase on plastic, make sure you understand the fees and costs up front!

can afford and grow in steps. Don't plan to fail. You may have been watching some late night show that told you to pyramid on plastic. But I'm telling you: *Don't do it.*

BUSINESS PLASTIC

A new kind of plastic is becoming available which could be the loan of the future. Lenders and finance companies are offering lines of credit which can be exercised by using plastic. While they promote it as if it is new, I can't find anything new about it. If you have good credit you can borrow money. Even though it is referred to as *unsecured borrowings*, you will most likely need to sign personally and/or pledge corporate assets as well. If the interest rate is high (or will soon get high), pass on this plastic, too.

SELLER FINANCING

Seller financing should not be the last on your list. It should be the first! Notwithstanding that the IRS will charge the seller an imputed interest rate for any money he loans a buyer, you can negotiate any terms and conditions you can get away with. My personal feeling is that you can get the best price and most cost-effective deal with cash. However, there is another theory that I also have confidence in. If you don't put any cash into the purchase and the business generates enough cash to pay all the bills, purchase money mortgage included, you can pay anything you want for the business. It really won't cost you anything. Of course you need to compensate yourself for your time and talent in the process but when the seller financing is retired there will be even more cash flowing.

What type of seller financing can you ask for? Any kind you can think of. Finance the inventory and I'll pay you the cost as it is sold. Lease me the equipment so I don't have to buy it, but give me an option to purchase it at a favorable price later. Loan me the down payment at a below market rate. Carry a one hundred percent mortgage on the real property at a favorable rate. Guarantee my bank loan. Take a second mortgage on my house instead of cash.

As in any transaction, you will negotiate more effectively if you take the time to learn the seller's goals. He may not need cash. He may prefer income. He may just need to get out of the business or out from under the pressure

**National Survey of
Small Business Finances, 1995**
Credit sources used by small firms

Traditional credit lenders

Traditional loan	54.8%
Commercial bank	36.9%
Finance company	11.6%
Leasing	7.6%

Nontraditional lenders

Owner loans	16.5%
Personal credit cards	39.1%
Business credit cards	27.7%

As firms grow, their reliance on the commercial banking system increases.

Source: Federal Reserve Board

I once bought a restaurant for no cash. I assumed certain liabilities of the business but I did not sign personally for any of them. The seller was most appreciative of my help, and we became good friends. She couldn't sleep at night because of the pressure of too much debt, and didn't want to work the business hours any more. She really didn't need the money. By the way, the restaurant generated enough cash to make all the payments — including the salary of the manager who ran the business for me.

of debt. Find out. Helping a seller achieve his goals does not have to cost you extra money.

Trying to find financing for a business purchase can be very frustrating. Lenders and investors want to put their money in the safest places possible. They may not tell you this right away, as they want a good relationship with you if your business venture is successful. A survey tabulated a few years ago is shown on this page, but it only relates the credit sources used by small firms. It does not specifically explain the sources used for the purchase of small firms. You need to investigate every possible source of financing. If more than one source is available to you, then compare the rates, terms, and conditions of each. This will be one of the most important business decisions you will make. Take your time.

Where Will You Raise Your Capital?

How probable is it that you will raise capital from the following sources?

Circle the comfort level for each issue.	High				Low
Savings	5	4	3	2	1
Relatives	5	4	3	2	1
Cash value of life insurance policies	5	4	3	2	1
Equity lines of credit	5	4	3	2	1
Equity partners	5	4	3	2	1
Investors	5	4	3	2	1
Banks	5	4	3	2	1
SBA guaranteed loan	5	4	3	2	1
SBICs	5	4	3	2	1
Mortgage brokers	5	4	3	2	1
Venture capital groups	5	4	3	2	1
Stock market	5	4	3	2	1
Plastic	5	4	3	2	1
Seller financing	5	4	3	2	1

About your answers: There are no right or wrong answers. Study your responses to determine which items you need help with. Have your spouse or potential partner(s) fill in a copy of the checklist also. Discovering which subjects lack high comfort levels will help you choose professionals with the appropriate skills.

"Without counsel purposes are disappointed;
but in the multitude of counselors they are established."

14

The Need for Professionals

- Legal
- Accounting
- Banking
- Practical Business People
- Investment Counselors/Brokers
- Build your Team

It is vital to assemble a team of professionals to assist you in your venture to buy or sell a business. Such a life-changing decision should not be made without adequate counsel. If you have a hole in your knowledge base, you won't even know it's there. Don't make the mistake of thinking you know all you need to know and have no use for advice. It's to your benefit! Get the professional assistance you need, but make the decisions yourself.

LEGAL

Any document that needs to be signed and witnessed should be reviewed by an attorney, if for no other reason than that you want to ensure you have an agreement that will not promote litigation. There is a distinction between legal advice and lawyer's advice. You don't need investment advice from a lawyer. You want your lawyer to check the document for legal sufficiency, looking for areas that are not clear in the agreement, or areas that are not clear in expressing the intent of the document.

Know what you are signing

Hiring a lawyer is no substitute for knowing what you are signing. If you don't clearly understand what is in the document, then get it explained to you. It is possible that a document which expresses clear intent between the parties will keep you out of court. Lawyers do not like to lose. Some of them will advise you not to go forward when they know you will lose in court.

Lawyers can overreact

Sometimes lawyers make mountains out of molehills — or use fear as a motivator to get you to agree with them. Lawyers are people, too — they put their pants on one leg at a time. Should you find yourself with a lawyer who attempts to use fear tactics on you, or who hasn't learned the difference between a small matter and a large matter, either straighten them out or find another professional.

Lawyers can be real deal killers

In over twenty years of experience in helping people buy and sell businesses, I keep thinking I have seen it all. Then I see something new and strange. Some of the strange changes are caused by lawyers who try to make decisions for their clients.

Your lawyer should coach you and counsel you. He should not be making any of your decisions. You do not need your lawyer to call a buyer or seller for you — to threaten or intimidate, and not even to negotiate. He might be the best person to talk directly with the other lawyer. But if feathers fly when they get near each other, you might want to reconsider who the best person is. Your need for counsel is not for serious litigation. You don't need a tiger to check your agreements for legal sufficiency — you need someone with wisdom and experience.

Lawyers will do what you ask

Just ask in advance. Never paint a lawyer into a corner. Be clear about what you want your lawyer to do and ask if he agrees with your plan of action. Discuss fees in advance. While it is true that an hourly rate is an industry standard, I do not often allow billing by this method. I would rather state the services needed and get a fee for the service. With a fixed fee, the job seems to get done more quickly. A good attorney who knows the subject could make more money with me by agreeing to the fixed fee. I just don't like to guess how much liability I am creating. I believe I already shared my power lunch strategy with you. Let your lawyer suggest the right lawyer.

ACCOUNTING

An experienced accountant should have more thorough knowledge and understanding of the numbers of businesses than almost anyone. Not only do they know the numbers for your business, but they have access to the numbers of their many clients. And they have access to publications that profile similar businesses and establish averages and ranges for sales and expenses — by geographic region.

Do I need a CPA? Yes — and no. What you need is an accountant with a good mind and an acceptable level of experience. Certainly, if you need audited statements, you will need the CPA. And in your locality, the best

mind might very well be the local CPA. The CPA is a committed person who has gone the extra mile to be the best in his or her profession. They have usually been subjected to a higher level of training. They should provide the highest level of quality services. You do not need a CPA to do your bookkeeping. In fact, they don't want to do it. Hire a bookkeeper to prepare the summaries used by accountants or CPAs.

Detached and objective
You might be surprised how you can lose your objectivity when you have made up your mind in advance. Your accountant can help protect you against incorrect suppositions. She should undo rosy projections.

Industry averages knowledge
You can either interview all similar business owners across the nation — or hire an accountant. They have access to this information. They even have access to the average numbers reported to the IRS for similar businesses. Not that they would encourage you to make up numbers to report, but they can point out when your numbers seem out of line. Then you can look to see if there is a problem.

Vision for future income streams
A seasoned accountant has seen a great variety of businesses in their growth stages and

can guide you through your stages. She may help you with a realistic expectation for future income streams. You don't have an accountant draw up your projections; you do the business plan and have the accountant check it.

Usually very conservative

Sometimes they can be too conservative. Accountants might not share your thoughts about cash flows, risk, leveraging, costs of capital, and other areas of business that involve decisions by you. That's okay. Those decisions are *your* decisions. If you are as conservative as an accountant, perhaps you should consider becoming one.

Help in packaging

Your accounting professional's name on your projections will help sell them. Have them "audit" your assumptions and then write their commentary on their letterhead. If you are not strong in this area, you might have the accountant do the projections and you do the audit.

Discuss fees in advance

As with any professional it is best to discuss fees before they are earned. Accurate expectations will allow your relationships with professionals to stay intact, or even grow. This will be a good time to find out what type of assignments your professional prefers to do and which jobs they really do

not want to do. If your professional does not want to discuss fees in advance, go shopping for another.

BANKING

It is not possible to run a business without banking relationships. Yes, that statement indicates the need for multiple banking relationships. I'm afraid that one bank won't do anymore. Banks are now specializing in their products and services. Charges and fees vary. Loan costs and returns on excess capital vary quite a bit. Go shopping for each product or service as needed.

Banks and other lenders are regulated on almost everything. If they make certain types of loans they may change their capital requirements, or possibly limit the amount they can lend. If loans get into trouble (default) they go into a different column. That's bad. If the loan does not fully conform to what the regulators want to see in the files, the loan is called a *nonconforming loan*. That's not good. At night they lie awake in fear of the *nonperforming, nonconforming loan*. That's the one that might cost them their job.

Vice president and up

You won't believe who banks will allow to talk to you about serious borrowing — people who do not even understand how an income statement works, or how it affects the balance sheet. The initial contact with any lender may very well be someone of this caliber. If the lender's representative is not clear about nor familiar with the information required in the file before the loan committee meets, or is not up on what the regulators require — you could lose days or even weeks in the funding process. Ask to speak with a vice president. If at all possible, have a mutual friend or business acquaintance introduce you to a banker with this title, prior to application for a loan. I am not sure what the title vice president means. I think in some banks it means he or she has been employed in the banking industry longer than one year.

If your bank's decisions are not made at your branch you may want to apply at the office where the loan committee meets. It will be the home office or the designated regional facility. Usually there is a capable commercial loan officer there.

Try your personal bank first

If you are operating a business already, you would first ask the people you bank with for any needed money. They know you. You are a depositor. Of course you might wind up changing banks in the process of finding a loan.

Wrong lending limits

Banks have lending limits. If a bank has a $350,000 lending limit, there isn't much point

street~smarts

Wrong time of the month. Be aware that banks "run out of money" often. They forecast their need to loan money. It's like your cash flow forecast — only in reverse. If they don't get the money out they are in big trouble. Sounds like fun, doesn't it? Seriously, when they lend their limits in any given time period, you don't want to be standing in line for a loan. You won't get it. The trick is to find out if they have money at the time you are applying — for the area of finance for which you are applying. Ask if they have any commercial money. Look for signals. If they ask you to come back for any reason, or you think they are stalling by continually asking for additional information, you might want to move on to another bank.

in asking for a $500,000 loan. Ask the lender what their commercial lending limit is. They will tell you they can work together with another bank to make the loan, but then you will be subject to the lending policies of two banks instead of one. It is better to apply at the bank with a higher lending limit. If you are in a rural area where all banks have low lending limits, an idea might be to break the cash needs down into smaller modules. One loan for real estate and one loan for equipment might be good reasoning.

Too much security required

In general, banks want all the collateral they can get to secure a commercial loan. This will most likely include the equity in your personal residence. Even though you have incorporated or formed an LLC to insulate yourself from undue liability against personal assets, a bank can override your actions by using those otherwise protected assets as security. Negotiate.

High front-end costs and fees

Don't pay costs or fees up front. If you need to pay any fees or costs associated with a commercial loan then request they be paid at the time of funding of the loan. Unscrupulous lenders can charge high front-end costs and then never fund the loan. Some make their living this way. Be aware.

You might need to shop for a loan

Similar to getting three bids for a construction job, go to two or three banks and tell them you are considering applying for a loan. Ask what the rates, terms, and conditions will be after you describe what the

street~smarts

A great idea is to have one of your professional team members make this inquiry for you. If your accountant or broker shops your loan request for you he will get a more objective answer. He will not need to divulge as much information to get the answers. This can work like a third party referral as he will actually be introducing you to the lender. If the lender hopes to have your professional bring more business to the bank, they will cooperate fully and be more open and honest.

loan request will be. Tell them you are checking with other lenders. Often the best rates are obtained in this manner.

PRACTICAL BUSINESSPEOPLE

Most people overlook the importance of relationships with other business owners. A good professional for your team will be someone who understands how your business operates and what your needs and desires are. Surround yourself with other business people. Get maximum input, but remember that you make your own decisions.

INVESTMENT COUNSELORS/BROKERS

There are agents — and also brokers. The difference is generally that an agent works for a broker. I believe you will be better off working with the broker. He makes the final decisions. You may find an independent broker who has no agents.

Each agent or broker has a tendency to specialize in areas that he or she feels comfortable with. The problem is that they do not like to turn away business, so they sometimes accept assignments that are not in their area of expertise. You should interview agents or brokers until you find the one who is right for your needs. It is not usual to find a good residential agent who will be good at commercial realty or business opportunity transactions. And vice versa. Ask those you interview for a short biography. Ask them to list the types of transactions they have completed successfully in the past year or two. Read them. Get personal references and check them.

Real estate agents/brokers are able to earn designations by taking series of courses in the fields they wish to pursue. In the commercial and industrial fields the respective top designations are Certified Commercial Investment Member (CCIM) and the Society of Industrial and Office Realtors (SIOR). The individuals who have earned these designations are the most highly educated in their professions. They generally

street~smarts

Who Are Business Brokers?

I don't know. Neither do you. Many states have no licensing requirement whatsoever for business brokers. That means they are not regulated. Their licenses cannot be revoked for dishonest business practices. There are no educational or experience requirements. I am not saying you cannot find a good business broker but you should never assume that he or she has any credentials. Interview and ask for the resume. Not the "nationally-known" business broker resume — the resume of the individual you are considering.

seek to be the best in their fields. Multiple designations do not necessarily indicate the best agent/broker. Either they have earned the designations on an upward path to reach the area in which they wish to specialize, or they like spending time in classes. There is no substitute for the resume. This will show you the experience level that goes with the designation.

It might be a good idea to consider hiring this professional as a consultant on a fee basis. Rather than tying the agent/broker's compensation to the completed transaction you may wish to pay an hourly rate for advice. If the agent/broker actually is the one who helps you purchase a business and/or real estate you may provide for additional compensation such as a normal brokerage fee. By hiring this professional as a consultant, you should increase the number of alternatives you have to reach your business goals. A consultant might help you set a selling price on your business, design a marketing strategy, and point you in the right direction for buying a business.

BUILD YOUR TEAM

Take the time to assemble your team of professionals. The relationships might go far beyond your initial transaction. Your team will guide you into the future. Your mission is to surround yourself with professionals that will help get you educated and keep you informed on all business matters you need to make your own decisions. (For more information on how to find a CCIM, see the appendix.)

How Do You Feel about your Professionals?

If this book is a library copy, please do not write in it. Photocopy this page instead.

Circle the comfort level for each issue.	High			Low	
Specialist in the right areas	5	4	3	2	1
Legal					
Good communicator	5	4	3	2	1
No mountains out of molehills	5	4	3	2	1
No deal-killer	5	4	3	2	1
Lets you make your own decisions	5	4	3	2	1
Affordable	5	4	3	2	1
Accounting					
Detailed and objective	5	4	3	2	1
Knows your industry	5	4	3	2	1
Lets you make your own decisions	5	4	3	2	1
Cooperative	5	4	3	2	1
Affordable	5	4	3	2	1
Banker/Financier					
Vice president & up	5	4	3	2	1
Your personal bank	5	4	3	2	1
Lending limits	5	4	3	2	1
Right time of month	5	4	3	2	1
Security required	5	4	3	2	1
Cash down required	5	4	3	2	1
Front-end costs & fees	5	4	3	2	1
Rates & terms	5	4	3	2	1
Amortization period	5	4	3	2	1
Practical business people	5	4	3	2	1

Continued on the next page

How Do You Feel about your Professionals?

If this book is a library copy, please do not write in it. Photocopy this page instead.

Continued from the previous page

Circle the comfort level for each issue.	High			Low	
	5	4	3	2	1
Counselor/Broker					
Experience	5	4	3	2	1
Knowledge	5	4	3	2	1
References	5	4	3	2	1

About your answers: There are no right or wrong answers. Study your responses to determine which items you need help with. Have your spouse or potential partner(s) fill in a copy of the checklist also. Discovering which subjects lack high comfort levels will help you choose professionals with the appropriate skills.

"Hear instruction, and be wise, and refuse it not."

15
More
street-smarts

I hope you've enjoyed street-smarts throughout the book. Here are a few more for your enjoyment and learning. Some are fun. Some will tickle your common sense. Some will make your brain work. Inhale them.

TURNAROUNDS
This is a good area for the real entrepreneur! Find a business that is doing poorly — even failing. Buy it and fix it. Sell it at a profit. Repeat. My premise here is that one who is good at business already has the necessary

skills and experience to ensure success in another business. If you have good gut instincts, you can pull off the turnaround. I know some people who do this and take a year off between ventures.

NOT ENOUGH PARKING

Let's say you find the perfect business to purchase. It is priced well. The business is generating a positive cash flow and will actually pay you a salary for management. You know you can introduce changes and improvements that will double the sales. Have you checked the parking available? When you double the sales there will be no place to park!

TAKE A JOB

Here is a good practical suggestion for those who plan to have a business, but do not have experience in that particular line of business. Get the experience first. Work in the field for a while. It can be part-time. Not only will you get an inside look at real operations and business conditions, you may find a few good employees (and customers). When you apply for financing it will help to list any type of experience in the field of business you plan to start or purchase.

HIRE THE BEST THE COMPETITOR HAS

I call this technique the double whammy. Not only do you get a good employee but you impact the competitor at the same time. Taking the new employee in to your confidence, you will learn all the trade secrets of the competitor, who the best customers are, what suppliers are the most dependable, and more about the general market than you could learn by yourself.

MAKE A PROFIT

I shouldn't have to say this. *Profit* is not a dirty word. You must make a profit — if for no other reason than to ensure you will be around next year to provide quality products or services to your favorite customers. There is an old saying that you can "make it on volume." Bull. What is zero profit on 10,000 sales? Purchase well. Price well. Market well. Make a profit.

WHAT'S YOUR RENT ESCALATION?

I helped a client buy a seafood carryout business a while back and a new lease needed to be signed by the buyer. I approached the landlord to determine what would be needed in the new lease and he was most helpful. He just wanted to keep the space rented. No increases in rents were needed, the insurance limits remained the same, and the tenant was acceptable to him. The one thing he did not want to do was pay me a fee to draw up the lease. This was fine with me; I wanted to represent the tenant/buyer. We offered a ten-year lease with no increases. No annual adjustments for Consumer Price Increases. Nothing. I took the time to explain to the landlord that the rent would remain constant for the entire term. He accepted the lease as written. His goals were to keep the space rented. Now five years later, the landlord sold his business that was operated from the same site. He's in the process of selling the entire property, part of which is my client's leasehold. New buyers of the property want to have my client's space back, but they must honor the lease for another five years. It is possible that my client will make more money from the sale of his lease rights than he could if he stayed there working for the next five years. He is going to take a short vacation – then open up a new seafood carryout business across the street.

REAL ESTATE NOT FOR SALE

I found the ideal location for my client's new business. It was just the right size building and was conveniently located to the market he wished to reach. There was only one problem: the building was not for sale. It was vacant, but the owner was not willing to sell. My client wanted to own the real estate from which he operated. What could we do now? I made an appointment with the owner and asked why he would not sell. He didn't want to pay a large amount of taxes on the capital gains a sale would generate, and because he was older, he needed income instead of cash. I explained to him that he didn't have any income since the building was vacant. He had risk instead of income. Then I explained that I would help him do a tax-deferred exchange into another property of the same approximate value as his – one that was fully leased to a Pizza Hut franchisee. They had eight years left on their lease and the owner saw this as a good deal. Talk about win-win! Because I am a commercial real estate broker, I made everybody happy and made an extra sale commission in the process!

THE CAR WASH TRANSACTION

When I was fairly new in the field of helping people buy and sell businesses, I was approached by a group that wanted to set up a car wash. They had identified a piece of property that was well-located for their use, but were having problems making a deal with the owner. They also needed help obtaining financing, permits, and finding a developer/builder that would complete the project. I took the assignment. The owner of the property was, in fact, hard to deal with. First of all, he didn't want to sell the land. He didn't want to develop it either. He just knew it was valuable, and that he should hang on to it. We talked about a ground lease for my clients — one with a term long enough for my clients to get a good return on their investment. The owner wanted each and every detail, but we were talking about a substantially technical legal transaction. Neither party wanted to be the first to hire an attorney to draw up the document. Here's what we did. I had the parties enter into a contract to enter into a ninety-nine-year ground lease at a specified annual rent, subject to the attorney for the owner/landlord's approval of a ground lease drawn by the attorney for the tenant. The parties negotiated the price and terms — the lawyers hammered out the details. It worked!

A MONTH-TO-MONTH LEASE
WILL STOP A SALE

I was asked to help a new client sell a bar business, but in the process of examining the seller's books and records, I found his lease was only month-to-month. I knew we could not find a buyer that would go along with the risk associated with losing one's lease on short notice. I asked the seller why he did not enter into a long-term lease, and he told me the owner would not allow it. Back to basics again. I made an appointment with the landlord. He wanted to sell the building and was afraid that a long-term lease might interfere with a sale. He felt no obligation to the tenant or the tenant's business. You can probably guess the happy ending. We offered the building and the business for sale as a package — and sold it in thirty days. If you will take the time to find out the goals of buyers and sellers — and landlords — you may find solutions to the most difficult problems.

VALUE VS. PRICE

Value and price are not the same. Well — not all the time. Something for sale will usually have a price. Whether you buy it or not depends on its value to you. When talking about the purchase of a business, different prospective purchasers might assign different values to it. Virtually anyone can assign values to equipment, inventory, and other assets, but a business is more than the total of all the asset values. It is an income producer. It has an image. It has a unique location. It may have trained employees. It may have good positioning in a competitive market. Whatever is unique about the business being considered, its value will appear different to each prospect. Why am I asking you to think about this?

I believe you should not be overly concerned with price. Instead, you should determine its value to you. Make any offers based on your value calculations. Remember when I said, "Price or terms"? Determine the goals of the seller and give him the terms he needs to reach those goals — at the lowest possible price. If you do this, you will increase your chances of being successful in the new business venture, since your initial costs can be lower.

By the way, a good question to ask a seller is, "How did you arrive at setting your selling price?" Sometimes the broker suggested it. Sometimes the seller based it on another sale that is not even similar enough to compare with yours. Sometimes they do not know. In any event, you may wind up with significant information that would not have been obtained by any other method.

street~smarts

Good, Fast, and Cheap:
Pick any two
Good and Fast? — Not Cheap
Good and Cheap? — Not Fast
Fast and Cheap? — Not Good

"The way of a fool is right in his own eyes:
but he that hearkeneth unto counsel is wise."

16
Sources of Help

The following sources may be of help as you plan and implement your business goals. You should develop your basic business plan and then inquire of each source to see if they are able and willing to help.

Neither the author nor the publisher endorses any of the following entities, although they are commonly used sources of help by others.

THE SERVICE CORP OF RETIRED EXECUTIVES (SCORE)

SCORE is a nonprofit organization that provides small business counseling and training under a grant from the Small Business Administration. SCORE members are successful retired business men and women who volunteer their time to assist aspiring entrepreneurs and small business owners. There are SCORE chapters in every state. For more information, visit: *www.score.org*

THE U.S. SMALL BUSINESS ADMINISTRATION (SBA)

The SBA, established in 1953, provides financial, technical, and management assistance to help Americans start, run, and grow their businesses. With a portfolio of business loans, loan guarantees, and disaster loans worth more than $45 billion, in addition to a venture capital portfolio of $13 billion, SBA is the nation's largest single financial backer of small businesses. Last year, the SBA offered management and technical assistance to more than one million small business owners. The SBA also plays a major role in the government's disaster relief efforts by making low-interest recovery loans to both homeowners and businesses.

America's twenty-five million small businesses employ more than fifty percent of the private work force, generate more than half of the nation's gross domestic product, and are the principal source of new jobs in the U.S. economy. Loads of information at their website: *www.sba.gov*

SBDCs

The SBA administers the Small Business Development Center Program to provide management assistance to current and prospective small business owners. SBDCs offer one-stop assistance to small businesses by providing a variety of information and guidance in central and easily accessible branch locations. The program is a cooperative effort of the private sector, the educational community, and federal, state, and local governments. It enhances economic development by providing small businesses with management and technical assistance. There is an office in each state. For more information, visit their website: *www.sba.gov/sbdc*

SBA'S ENTREPRENEURIAL DEVELOPMENT PROGRAM

The mission of the SBA's Entrepreneurial Development Program is "To help small businesses start, grow, and be competitive in global markets by providing quality training, counseling, and other forms of management and technical assistance." Visit their web site: *www.sba.gov/ed*

BUSINESS INFORMATION CENTERS (BICs)

These centers are part of the SBA network of help for business owners. They loan books and videotapes and present training workshops on starting and expanding your business. *www.sba.gov*

BANKERS

I know I haven't said a lot of nice things about bankers in this book, but they are still a source worth investigating. You will need a very solid business plan to present. Your plan should include a detailed description of the business and its goals, a discussion of the ownership of the business and the legal structure contemplated, a list of the skills and experience you bring to the business, and the advantages you and your business have over your competitors. You will need to state clearly how much financing you need and the uses you plan for the money. In my experience, bankers will not accept much risk at all. If they don't respond favorably to your submission, you need to find out why. You may need to adjust your business plan to make it more acceptable. They may be looking for some secondary method of repayment of any loan in case the business does not do as well as expected. Bank financing may not the solution for you, but it won't

hurt to seek feedback from one or two of them.

ACCOUNTANTS

Not all accountants really have a head for business. That's okay — you are not asking them to make your decisions for you. What you want them to do is comment on your business plan, the projected cash flows, the anticipated expenses, and so forth, and to point out anything that appears out of order. With their experience with many small businesses, they will notice things in your plan that raise questions. Spend some time with them, and get them to open up and be free with their observations and questions.

BETTER BUSINESS BUREAUS

It's always a good idea to see if there are complaints on file with this source. They don't have as much information as you would hope, but if you're considering a bad apple, you may find out about it here.

CHAMBERS OF COMMERCE

You don't go there because they have the answers. You go there because they are a strong network of area businesspeople who are resources. You may ask them to refer you to one of their members, or even to introduce you to the person who may have answers to your specific questions. Make sure you mention that you plan to enroll in their chamber when your business is up and running. By the way, most chambers put together a package of area demographics that are invaluable in planning. They also have a good handle on the competition (or lack thereof) in your area. Ask.

UNIVERSITIES' SCHOOLS OF BUSINESS

Not many people know this, but universities with schools of business are usually open to projects for their students to work on. You may have to pay for their services or supplies, but it will be *much* less expensive than hiring a consultant to do the work. They are especially good at conducting inexpensive market research.

TRADE ASSOCIATIONS' JOURNALS

Most every business or industry has a trade magazine associated with the specific field of business. Ask around until you find what's available, then get copies and scour them for needed information. Your library may have back issues with articles that will make you smarter and more prepared to make your plans work. Get abreast of current or anticipated changes in your business area. See what others feel is worthy to write about. Get information.

OTHER BUSINESSPEOPLE

If you interview successful business owners about your business plan or product/service markets, you will discover information that may not be available from other sources. What I suggest is that you go out of the geographic area you plan for your business and ask for advice. If you let them know you do not plan to compete with them, most will be flattered you feel their advice is worth asking for. They're just people. Here are some sample questions you might ask: Are there slow times of year for this business? Any particular cash flow problems associated with this industry? What's looming on the horizon? What legislation is pending that might affect your business venture? Buy them lunch. Tell them you need their help. Treat them like people.

SERVICE CLUBS

These are groups of businesspeople that are taking the time to get together over meals to help each other and address community needs. For the most part, they are very nice people and some will be anxious to help you. The Rotary club in your area is worth a visit. They believe in furthering their particular vocations (it's one of their goals) and that's what you will be giving them the opportunity to do. When your business is up and running, consider being part of one or more of these valuable clubs. If not for the potential extra business, join to give back to your community. Network!

INTERNET

This book has not addressed businesses that specialize in marketing over the Internet because that subject would fill an entire volume. A chapter wouldn't even be a teaser. You must learn to utilize the Internet resources. Learn to use search engines and sites. If you are not computer literate, find or hire someone who is. You can learn just about anything you can think of or find answers to any question online. There are discussion groups in so many places that I won't don't begin to mention them. Well — okay — try the *New York Times* website: *www.nytimes.abuzz.com*. Here you can interact with others and even ask specific questions about business. When you receive an answer (they will send you an e-mail if you request it), you can click on the sender's name and get a personal history of the source (assuming they registered one at the site).

LIBRARIES

Libraries have become more sophisticated in recent years. Even small community libraries can network with regional facilities to obtain books. If they don't have the book on their shelves, they will order it for you from another library.

Personally, I buy the books and keep them in my personal library as reference materials. If you borrowed this book, photocopy the order form in the back of the book and get your own copy. *Order a copy for a friend*!

CLIENTS

Especially if you are in a service business, you should interview your clients and ask questions about your business plan. You should be fully aware of clients' needs and problems. If you are going to be successful, you must fill needs and solve problems for your clients. That will keep them coming back for more. Learn all you can about what is important to them.

CUSTOMERS

For retail and wholesale businesses, who better to feed you the market research? What do they like about your (prospective) product or service line? What turns them off? How much can they afford to pay for just the right offerings? What makes them loyal? How can you earn and keep their business?

FRIENDS (EVEN RELATIVES)

You cannot follow all the advice you get from friends and relatives — and some may expect you to do so. Weighing the cost, it is still advisable to poll these nice people to get ideas about your prospective business venture. You may need their help to get where you're going. Nobody really does it alone, you know. They may be your financier before it's over. They will be the ones to encourage you when you're blue. They may be needed to answer phones when your growth explodes. They may just need to know that they are valuable to you. Talk to them.

Appendix

- Miscellaneous Resources
- Business Forms
- Software and Publications
- Other Information Sources
- Websites

These resources are intended to provide helpful and informative material on the subject matters covered in this book. If the reader requires personal assistance or advice, a competent professional should be consulted. These resources are offered without guarantee on the part of the author or streetsmartbooks, LLC. The author and streetsmartbooks, LLC, specifically disclaim any responsibility for any liability, loss or risk, personal or otherwise, which is incurred as a consequence, directly or indirectly, of the use and/or application of any of the resources listed herein.

MISCELLANEOUS RESOURCES

Find a CCIM (Certified Commercial Investment Member).

For a complete directory on CD-ROM, call the CCIM Institute: 312-321-4460, or visit the web site and search by City/State: www.ccim.com

BUSINESS FORMS

- Business purchase contract(s) available at:
  www.streetsmartbooks.com

- NOI calculation sheet available at:
  www.streetsmartbooks.com

- Buyer Broker Rep. Agreement available at :
  www.streetsmartbooks.com

SOFTWARE AND PUBLICATIONS

- *The Complete Book of Small Business Legal Forms*
  by Daniel Sitarz,
  Attorney-at-Law,
  Nova Publishing Company,
  Carbondale, IL.
  1-800-748-1175
     Includes book & disk

- *BizComps*
  Business Brokerage analyses and valuations.
  www.bizcomps.com

- *Annual Statement Studies*
  by Robert Morris Assoc.
  Philadelphia, PA.
     Available in book form or on disk. Lists businesses by SIC codes. RMA Publishers
     800-677-7621

OTHER INFORMATION SOURCES

- Consumer Information Center
  P.O. Box 100
  Pueblo, CO 81002
     Offers a consumer information catalog of federal publications.

- Government Printing Office, Superintendent of Documents, Washington, DC 20402-9328
     Request a subject bibliography. GPO bookstores are located in twenty-four major cities and are listed in the Yellow Pages under the bookstore heading.

- Small Business Answer Desk, Small Business Administration
  800-U-ASK-SBA (827-5722)

- U.S. Department of Commerce (DOC), Office of Business Liason
  Room 5898C
  14th Street & Constitution Avenue, NW, Washington, DC 20230
    Their Business Assistance Center provides listings of business opportunities available in the federal government. Also helps with referrals to other programs and services.

- U.S. Department of Labor
  Employment Standards Admin.
  200 Constitution Avenue, NW, Washington, DC 20210
    Offers publications on compliance with labor laws.

- Internal Revenue Service
  U.S. Dept. of Treasury
  P.O. Box 25866
  Richmond, VA 23260.
    Offers information on tax requirements for small businesses.

- *Franchise Opportunities Guide*
  International Franchise Assoc (IFA)
  1-800-543-1038 or visit:
  www.franchise.org

WEBSITES

- **www.streetsmartbooks.com**
  My publisher — lots of good stuff!

- **www.sba.gov**
  Small Business Administration — good links!

- **www.census.org**
  U.S. Census Bureau

- **www.instbusapp.org**
  Institute of Business Appraisers

- **www.inc.com**
  Inc. Magazine

- **www.sbaloans.com**
  Business Loan Express

- **smallbusiness.yahoo.com**
  Yahoo Business Site

- **www.businessweek.com**
  Business Week

- **www.entrepreneurmag.com**
  Entrepreneur

- **www.forbes.com**
  Forbes

- **www.fortune.com**
  Fortune

- **www.money.com**
  Money

- **businessdirectory.dowjones.com**
  Wall Street Journal

- **www.bizcomps.com**
  Database on completed transactions

- **www.bizbuysell.com**
  Service for business brokers, buyers, and sellers

Glossary

A

acceptance

An offer to sell or purchase a business is not valid until all parties sign the document(s) and the document is delivered to all parties. Upon full execution (signatures) and delivery, the offer is accepted.

active income

A designation of the IRS. This manner of income requires material involvement in the production of the income. Active income does not generally include rental income.

additional rents

A term used in leases that causes payment obligations other than the base rent to become "rents." A court will usually not grant a money judgment for payments other than rents, so it is a good practice for a landlord to designate all payments from tenants to be rents.

allocation of purchase price

A determination of the manner in which the purchase price should be assigned to each item that is included in the purchase price. An amount will usually be assigned to assets, inventory, and so forth. Since the allocation will affect both the buyer's and seller's tax consequences, it is an object of negotiation.

amortization

The process of liquidating a debt through installment payments. Also, prorating expenditures over time in order to write them off.

angel

A private investor who often has non-monetary motives for investing as well as the usual financial ones.

annual debt service (ADS)

The annual outlay for principal and interest on debt.

arbitration

A form of conflict resolution in which a neutral third party hears both parties' arguments and renders a decision.

assumption

When one party takes over the rights or obligations of another.

audit(ed)

Examination of an individual's or organization's records in an attempt to verify accuracy and legal compliance. This should be done by a CPA.

B

balance sheet

An accounting statement showing the financial condition of a company at a point in time — assets, liabilities, and net worth. The sheet declares the total assets, deducts the total liabilities, and calculates the resulting net worth.

basis

A value assigned to all property by the IRS (Internal Revenue Service) for tax purposes. It is usually determined by taking the purchase price of a business (or asset), plus any capital improvement invested in the business, and deducting the accumulated depreciation. When a business is sold, the taxable amount is the price less the basis.

bills of sale

Written agreements stating the terms by which ownership of goods is transferred to another party.

book value

The value of an asset as reflected in the books of the company owning the item. This value is the cost of the asset less any depreciation taken against it.

brown out

A condition in which a person has materially slowed down or lost interest in the business.

bulk sales transfer

A requirement in the sale of a business. The pending sale is publicly advertised to give notice to creditors, and a filing is made that is used for the basis of sales and other taxes.

burnout

A condition is which a person has lost both energy and objectivity in the business. This condition often leads to business failure.

business broker

A person/agent who helps other people buy and sell businesses. This person may or may not have credentials or experience in the field. A license may not be required.

buyer's broker representation agreement

A contract between a business broker and a principal interested in buying a business. While terms and conditions are negotiable, the document usually describes the duties and obligations of the broker and terms of payment for the broker's services.

buy-sell agreement

A promise among partners that when one owner desires to sell his interest he will first offer it for sale to the other owners. A contract between associates that sets the terms and conditions by which one or more of the associates can buy out one or more of the other associates. It is an accepted practice for a business to secure life insurance policies on each of the principals in order to generate cash to buy out a partner's interest if he dies. A means of protecting principal parties in a venture from undue financial loss should the personal and/or business relationships among the founders or investors disintegrate. This agreement saves aggravation, legal expenses, and goodwill. It is a wise provision inserted into agreements between private investors and entrepreneurs that also allows them to get rid of troublesome investors.

C

capital

A term commonly used as a synonym for cash. Capital goods are material assets, equipment, machinery, or tools. Capital funds is also cash.

capitalization rate

The determination of the value of a

property based on the rate of return on the investment in the property.

capital requirements

Cash needed, spent, or sought to invest for the purpose of making more money. Also known as investment capital.

cash flow

The most important consideration of business survival. The measurement of the differences between the actual cash received by a firm and its actual cash expenditures. Only the flow of cash is measured. Noncash transactions such as depreciation, amortization, credit sales, and purchases on account are ignored.

cash flow after tax

The calculation of cash flow after consideration of expected or actual payments for income and other taxes.

cash flow before tax

The net income generated by conducting business with a deduction made for interest owed/paid on company debts.

cash flow forecast

A report prepared to anticipate whether the operation will generate positive or negative cash flow. Used to determine how much cash will be needed or generated for a specific period of time.

cash on cash return after tax

A formula that calculates the return on investment and includes the payment of income taxes due.

cash on cash return before tax

A formula that calculates the return on investment that does not consider the tax consequences.

cash position

The amount of cash immediately available (short-term) for use in the operation of the business.

cash value of life insurance

Also known as cash surrender value, this is the amount an insurance company would pay the policyholder during his or her lifetime when the life insurance policy is terminated. Taking this cash and canceling the insurance policy is known as "cashing in."

Certified Commercial Investment Member (CCIM)

A designation awarded by the CCIM Institute to those persons who have completed stipulated courses in various phases of commercial real estate activity and demonstrated competence in all areas of the course subject matter. Considered the Ph.D. of commercial real estate.

Certified Development Companies (CDC)

Public-private investment groups that are interested in fostering business in their communities.

Certified Public Accountant (CPA)

An accountant who has met all of a state's requirements and has received a state certificate.

compromise with creditors

An agreement between the debtor and creditors to pay a reduced sum or stipulated payments to satisfy debt. This agreement is based upon good faith promises by the debtor and usually will not adversely affect the credit rating. Collection efforts usually will be suspended or terminated upon the agreement.

conditioned upon

A legal term that may be used in written agreements that limits the performance of the agreement to the completion of items that are declared to be "conditions." If a condition cannot or is not met, the agreement can be voided or terminated, depending on the terms of the agreement.

confidentiality statement; also known as nondisclosure agreement

A legal agreement stipulating that the signee not disclose confidential information about the company and/or product; purchasers, employees, consultants, contractors, and sometimes vendors are often required to sign nondisclosure agreements. These cover not just proprietary technology, formulas, and the like, but also business strategies, marketing plans, client and customer lists, financial information, and trade secrets.

Consumer Price Index (CPI)

A measure of inflation used in the United States, calculated by the U.S. Bureau of Labor Statistics.

contingency

A legal term that may be used in written agreements that declares an issue that must be met or satisfied for the agreement to remain fully enforceable.

contract; also known as a purchase agreement

A promise or a set of promises for breach of which the law gives a remedy, or the performance of which the law in some way recognizes as a duty.

corporate acknowledgment

The signature and seal affixed to an agreement that attests to the corporation's affirmation and acceptance of the agreement. Also a form that evidences that permission to contract or act was voted upon in a meeting of the board of directors.

corporation

A legal entity created under state law. A form of organization wherein ownership is vested in the stockholders. Chief Justice John Marshall's classic definition (1819) reads: A corporation is an official being, invisible, intangible, and existing in contemplation of law. Being the mere creature of law, it possesses only those properties which the charter of its creation confers upon it, either expressly, or as incidental to its very existence. These are such as the same, and may act as a single individual. They enable a corporation to manage its own affairs, and to hold property without the perplexing intricacies, the hazardous and endless necessity, of perpetual conveyances for the purpose of transmitting it from hand to hand. It is chiefly for the purpose of clothing bodies of men, in succession, with these qualities and capacities, that corporations were invested, and are in use.

counter offer

A change or changes made to an offer. Making a counter offer automatically voids the original offer.

covenant not to compete; also known as a noncompete agreement

A promise not to compete with another as evidenced by a written agreement. The covenant usually specifies the limits to be honored — usually by business type and geography. It may limit one's ability to be involved in another similar or competing business, or even to be financially involved in another business by way of investment.

customer base

A business's known customers, usually defined by a written list.

D

debt financing

Financing that is given without ownership rights to a business. This financing may or not be secured by a pledge of assets.

deposits; also know as earnest money

Payment in advance showing the serious intent of a buyer; the amount is usually a part of the purchase price. Sometimes called front money. Depending on the wording of the agreement, a deposit may be forfeited by a purchaser under certain circumstances, such as nonperformance.

depreciation

The periodic allocation of the cost of a tangible long-lived asset over its estimated useful life. Land cannot be depreciated because it has unlimited life. Used in the determination of income tax liability and profit and loss calculation.

distress

A condition or perception of a condition that indicates a business is not operating properly. A variety of reasons will lead to distress, and any distress will cause a loss of value (price) to a seller of a business.

down time

Nonproductive period of time. Down time will be encountered in a business startup or during times when a business is forced to cease operations temporarily.

due diligence

A form of research; a reasonable investigation conducted by the parties involved, usually part of the performance of an agreement to purchase.

E

enhancement

Changing the nature of a business to add value. This can be done through expansion, change of product lines, adding or training employees, and so forth.

entrepreneur

Derived from the French word "to undertake." Someone who is willing and eager to create a new venture in order to present a concept to the marketplace. An entrepreneur is one who creates and manages change by pursuing opportunity and acting on it.

entrepreneurship

A process through which individuals and groups pursue opportunity, leverage resources, and initiate change to create value.

equity financing

Funds invested in a business by its owners or by investors who become owners through terms and conditions of the financing.

equity mortgage

Invested funds secured by real property by those who are owners or who become owners through the terms and conditions of the note and mortgage.

equity partner

A part owner who has invested money or assets in a business.

equity rate of return

The return on investment of capital by owners.

escrow

Placing money in a special and separate account under the control of another party, to be held until the completion of conditions set forth in an agreement. This term is also used to describe the activities of the other party to effect verification of the terms and conditions of an agreement and the handling of settlement details.

escrow account funds

Money that is placed into trust with a third party.

estoppel

A written document executed by a tenant that verifies his rents, lease terms, and conditions. It usually certifies that he has no uncompleted obligations due him from the landlord.

excess over basis; also known as goodwill

The difference between the market value of a firm and the market value of its net tangible assets.

expense (expensing)

Items which are paid that affect the profit and loss of a business. These are generally all but capital items, and sometimes exclude owners' salaries and benefits that are actually part of the profit/loss of the business.

F

fees

Money due to brokers, consultants, and contractors for services rendered. These are always negotiable. They are due and payable depending upon the terms and conditions of the agreement between the parties.

filing statements

Administrative paperwork required to be filed by franchises in most states. These statements are available for public review. States place strict burdens of proof on the franchise's use of any financial information or data.

financial management rate of return (FMRR)

A calculation of return on investment, adjusted for the time value of money that includes the reinvestment of positive cash flow over the period of time for which the calculation is made.

financial strength

The net worth of the individual or company.

first right of refusal

A written agreement that gives one party the right to purchase or rent property before any other party may do so. This right is triggered by an offer to lease or purchase by another party, after which the owner or landlord must offer the right to lease or purchase to the primary party. Terms and conditions of the rights offered will be those specifically described in the written agreement.

foreign entity

Any business, corporation, or entity that operates in any state in which it is not domiciled or incorporated.

form 940

The quarterly report to the IRS that files information about employees, payroll, and withholding taxes.

form 941

The annual report that combines all four quarters of the form 940 reporting.

franchise

A contract between two parties. In modern usage, it is a license from the franchiser that entitles its holder to operate a particular type of business according to certain stated conditions and arrangements.

front-end costs or fees

Fees paid prior to the application or completion of the provisions of financing, purchasing, or the providing of services. Payment of these costs or fees should be avoided whenever possible.

furniture and fixtures; also know as furnishings, fixtures, and equipment. (FFE) (1) An item, such as a display counter or a rack, that is used as an aid to help in the buying or selling process; (2) an item that cannot be removed easily without damaging the property because it is attached to a building. Once attached, a fixture usually becomes part of the property. Attachment of trade fixtures usually does not transfer ownership.

G

goodwill; also known as excess over basis
The difference between the market value of a firm and the market value of its net tangible assets.

government approvals
An approval required by any government or quasi-governmental authority to construct, occupy, or use a property, or to engage in a specific activity.

graduated rents
A schedule of future rents that are negotiated and agreed to in advance.

grandfathered
An existing business or real estate condition that was in effect prior to the passage of more strict rules or regulations. The term indicates that the nonconforming feature of the business or real estate is permitted to remain, but use may be lost under certain circumstances, such as change of ownership, or damage to or changes to the business or property.

gross rents
Rents that include all payment obligations in one monthly amount. In some circumstances, gross rents may even include utilities.

I

imputed interest rate
A rate set by the IRS that will be considered the interest rate owed or paid under certain circumstances. If the financing provider does not charge enough interest to a borrower, the IRS will declare the interest rate is counted to be (imputed) a higher rate for income tax purposes.

incentive-motivated
Any reward, whether monetary or psychological, that motivates and/or compensates an employee or manager for performance above standard.

income approach
A method used to appraise the value of a business or real property, based upon the income and expenses of the business or property.

internal rate of return (IRR)
A measure of an investment's performance that determines cash return ad-

justed for the time value of money. The rate is expressed as a percentage.

inventory

The quantity of goods on hand that are available for use or resale.

investment base

The amount of capital invested in a business or real property. This amount will include the price and any other costs involved in the purchase or acquisition.

investment counselor

Any person who offers opinions or advice to an investor or purchaser of a business. The use of this title does not guarantee any training, experience, or business license.

J

joint venture

Usually refers to a partnership with each partner sharing in costs and rewards of the project, but can describe any agreement in which two or more parties or entities agree to be involved.

L

lease

A form of contract that conveys to another the right to possess property in return for payment, usually in the form of rent. In a lease, the person who conveys the property is the landlord/lessor and the person who holds the property under a lease is the tenant/lessee. A lease must be in writing to be enforceable.

lease assignment

The transfer of lease rights and obligations from one person (the assignor) to another person (the assignee). Items other than leases can be assigned, such as sales contracts, mortgages, options, and property.

leasehold

The premises and the rights granted to a tenant under a lease agreement.

leasehold improvement

An improvement to leased property, considered an intangible asset to the lessee, that becomes the property of the lessor at the end of the lease. Some leases require the removal of the improvements at the end of the lease at the tenant's cost and that the premises be restored to their original condition.

legal sufficiency

A term used to describe the effectiveness of a legal document. All legal documents should be reviewed by an attorney to find terms or conditions that might give rise to future litigation, or that are not appropriate or normal for the transaction.

letter of credit

A bank's written guarantee of funds

available for drafts written on it.

liabilities

Debts of the business or individual; amounts owed or obligations to perform services to creditors, employees, government bodies, or others; claims against assets.

limited liability company (LLC)

A type of business formation that allows the owners to be taxed as an individual or partnership, but with the limited liability of a corporation. A similar entity is the limited liability partnership. The requirements and attributes of LLCs or LLPs vary from state to state.

line of credit

Short-term financing usually granted by a bank up to a predetermined limit; debtor borrows as needed up to the limit of credit without need to renegotiate the loan.

liquidated damages

The funds, referred to in a sales contract, that the buyer forfeits if he or she fails to go through with the contract. A liquidated damages clause in an agreement usually leaves no other recourse, such as court action.

liquidation

The process of converting assets into cash.

M

market comparison

A method used by appraisers to determine the value of a business or real estate. This method bases the value on other sales of the same type of business or property, or similar sales in the general geographic area.

market gap

A demand for products or services in a geographic area that is not being met by local vendors.

markups

The difference between what the customer and the retailer pay for goods. Usually expressed as a percentage and added to the cost of a product/service to determine its retail price.

month-to-month

An agreement that automatically terminates at the end of each month unless both parties agree to extend it.

mortgage broker

An individual or firm that represents more than one lender whose job is to find borrowers for the lenders.

N

net operating income (NOI)

The profit (loss) generated by a business that subtracts all expenses from the sales. In a small business, this is the profit for the owners. NOI is usually calculated before the payment of income taxes and debt service.

net proceeds of sale

The money a seller receives after the expenses of the sale.

net worth

The actual dollar value of the total owners' investment in a business plus any net profits that have been retained in the business from year to year. Determined on the balance sheet by subtracting liabilities from assets.

noncompete agreement

A legal agreement(s) stipulating that the signee will not join, start, or finance a similar or competing venture.

nonconforming loan

Any loan that cannot readily be sold on the secondary market.

nonconforming use

A use that does not comply with current zoning or other governmental rules or regulations. The permission to operate as or stay as a nonconforming use may terminate under certain circumstances.

nonperforming loan

A loan that is not current in its payment obligations.

nontransferable

An agreement that is not allowed to be transferred by its terms or conditions.

notification

One party's notice to another. Legal notification should be in writing and sent by certified mail, return receipt requested, to the other party's known address. Certain public recordings or advertisements fulfill the legal requirements of notification.

O

obsolescence

A diminishing of a product's usefulness and attraction usually due to the introduction of new and improved items that perform better, are less expensive, or both. Technical obsolescence occurs because of a new, superior technology or innovation.

overhead

Operating cost not directly associated with the product or its marketing, such as rent, managers' salaries, administrative expenses, and so forth.

P

packaging

The task of putting material together for prospects when you sell your business. The end result, the sales package, is used by brokers and others helping you find prospects; it contains the information and representations upon which buying decisions are made. The amount of detail and information you include is according to your personal preference.

paralegal

Persons trained to aid lawyers but not licensed to practice law.

partnership

A business association of two or more people. Partnership is a very general term that can be used to describe an association of virtually any type. The two primary types of partnerships are general and limited. In a general partnership, partners usually share in both management and financial liability. In a limited partnership, all but the general (managing) partner are usually only liable to the extent of their cash investments in the operation. Profits and tax benefits are divided according to prior agreement.

partnership agreement

The document used to specify the rights and obligations of each partner, including the management and distribution of profits or losses. The agreement should be in writing and should be reviewed from time to time.

passive income

Income designated by the IRS to be passive is that income derived from sources where you are not materially involved in the day-to-day operation that generates the income. Rental income is deemed to be passive income unless you can meet the IRS criteria for assigning it to active income status.

performance mortgage

The recorded document that pledges real property under a performance note.

performance note

An agreement to pay money based on the performance of stated events or operations. For example, a seller might grant a performance note that states payments will only be made when and if the business generates a profit.

personal property

All property that is not real property, or attached to real property. Examples of personal property are furnishings, equipment, trade fixtures, and inventory.

personalty

Another name for personal property.

plastic

As used in this book, the term means credit or debit cards.

platform concept

An ongoing business. The concept indicates that there is a value to a business that is already established (as opposed to starting a similar business).

possession

To have control over, such as a leased

premises. It is possible to have possession without ownership — even with a business. It is risky to allow someone to have unregulated possession of anything you own.

preferred lender

Status of certain lenders who package loans that are to be guaranteed by the SBA. These lenders actually make the lending decisions. Funding is subject to SBA's final approval.

price

The sum of money (or equivalent) for which something is bought or sold.

A price can include money, promises to pay (debt), exchanges, or equity.

principal paydown

Mortgage payments include both principal and interest. Each time a payment is made, some of the principal is repaid. The paydown is the amount the principal is reduced over a given period of time.

private records

As used in this book, this means records that are not required to be kept by government agencies or normally accepted accounting procedures. Private records are sometimes kept by individuals that have two sets of books for the purpose of deception. Extreme care should be taken when dealing with someone who does this.

profit

What results from revenues when all expenses have been paid.

profit and loss (statement)

A financial statement that shows the amount of income earned by a business over a specific accounting period. All costs (expenses) are subtracted from the gross revenues (sales) to determine net income, which outlines the profit and loss financial statement (P & L). These statements can be either audited or unaudited.

prorations

Costs that span a period of time that continue through a change of ownership are apportioned between the buyer and seller. The dividing of the costs is called prorating. Each pays his appropriate share of the costs.

portability

As used in this book, this is the ability to move a business to a different location.

purchase agreement

The contract used to buy and sell a business.

R

recovery of investment

The return of capital that has been invested, usually through the use of the asset and tax savings through depreciation. Most business assets are expected to be recovered over either their useful life or the term over which they are depreciated. A sale can recover the investment in its entirety.

rent escalation

The amount by which rent changes from term to term. Two ways for rent to increase without annual negotiating are by the use of graduated rents or by adjusting the rent according to changes in the Consumer Price Index.

rents

The cost to possess leased space.

replacement cost

The amount of money it would take to replace an asset, inventory, or property at current costs.

resale merchandise; inventory

The quantity of goods that are on hand available for resale.

rescind

To cancel an offer before it has been accepted and delivered back to you.

return on assets (ROA)

A measurement of a company's ability to produce net profits by effectively utilizing its assets. The higher the ratio, the more effective the company is at using its assets to produce profits.

return on equity (ROE)

A measurement of the return on the owner's investment in the company. Perhaps the most important measure of a business' financial viability. The higher the ratio, the higher the rate of return on the owner's investment.

return on investment (ROI)

A measurement of the amount of money that has been realized as a result of a certain investment of resources. The amount earned in proportion to the capital invested, usually stated as a percentage.

return on sales (ROS)

A measurement of the percent of every dollar in sales that a company maintains as net profit after all direct and indirect expenses are paid. The higher the ratio, the more profits being captured from each dollar of sales.

reversibility

As used in this book, this is the ability, according to a business plan, to get out of an undesirable or failing situation.

risk

The possibility that something can go wrong, or not according to plan. It is almost impossible to measure risk, although there is a term called *calculated risk*. The amount of risk each person can tolerate is different.

S

S corporation; also known as a sub-chapter S corporation

A firm that has elected to be taxed as a partnership under the sub-chapter S provision of the Internal Revenue Code.

SBA guaranteed loan

A loan for which the SBA promises to repay a portion if the loan is not repaid according to its terms and conditions. The most common source of SBA financing is the 7(a) loan guaranty, which is obtained through a lender and receives a guarantee of repayment from the SBA (the collateral holder).

SBDC - Small Business Development Centers

Centers administered by the SBA that provide management assistance to current and prospective business owners through one-stop assistance.

SBIC - Small Business Investment Company

A firm that provides equity capital, long-term loans, debt-equity investments, and management assistance to qualifying small businesses through a program of the Small Business Administration. Small Business Investment Companies are licensed investment firms that use private capital along with SBA-backed debentures to help finance small businesses.

season (seasoning)

To keep alive for a period of time. A seasoned note is one that has been in existence for a year or more. A seasoned business is one that has survived for three or more years. A seasoned business or note seems safer to an investor or lender.

seller financing

A general term that indicates a seller has taken or will take something other than all cash for his business. Seller financing can be your down payment to qualify for a bank loan, the proceeds of which you would give to the seller. If other financing is also used in connection with the purchase of a business, the seller may be the junior loan, and subject to the bank loan's successful repayment.

servicing debt

The process of collecting and processing payments made on loans. When loans are sold, it is usual for the lender that made the loan to continue servicing the debt.

slippage

The amount of sales of goods or services that are not being spent in the local market because customers are spending their money in another geographic area.

Society of Office and Industrial Realtors (SIOR)

A designation of the National Association of Realtors earned by those who receive training and qualify for the title. Areas of specialty are the creation and leasing of office space and industrial square footage.

sole proprietorship

One of the simplest forms of business. An individual is the owner of the business and has full responsibility for its operation and is entitled to all profits as well as liabilities and losses. A business firm owned by only one person and operated for his/her profit.

small business

A commercial enterprise that, as defined in the federal Small Business Administration Act, is independently owned and operated and which is not dominant in its field of operation. An agricultural enterprise is considered a small business by the SBA if it (including its affiliates) has annual receipts not in excess of $500,000. Other definitions, for such purposes as taxation or employee benefits, may be based on such factors as the number of employees or the amount of annual revenue.

subject to

A legal term that can be inserted into a contract that makes the contract cancelable or voidable if the condition cannot be met, or is not met.

sugardaddy

Another term for an angel or private investor. A relative that invests in your business can be your sugardaddy.

supplements

Pages that become part of your contract when you add them; usually at the end of the contract. Any term or condition that requires special treatment or is not covered in the main body of the contract can become a supplement.

T

terms

Any condition, period of time, right to inspect or investigate, or item that is a part of the agreement is a term.

time is of the essence

A legal term that means all dates are exactly as stated in the agreement and can only be changed if both parties agree. An action that is one day late is a default. No extensions or flexibility of time are allowed.

time value of money

All money commands interest, either imputed or explicit. Interest costs are a function of the interest rate and the time for which the money is being rented (used). Thus time costs money.

trade association

A not-for-profit organization that exists to support its members. Usually, those that belong to a trade association work in closely related occupations.

trade fixtures

Items commonly used in a business that may be or may not be attached to the real property. Courts generally hold that trade fixtures, even when attached to real property, continue to be the property of the tenant.

trade name

A name used by a manufacturer or merchant for a product. A trade name for a company or business that is not the legal company or business name is called a "fictitious name."

transition plan

A plan of action that outlines the rights and responsibilities of the parties during the period of time the business is undergoing change of ownership.

triple-net (NNN)

A description of a lease that provides for the tenant to pay extra amounts monthly to pay for, or reimburse the owner for, real estate taxes, hazard insurance, and maintenance of the grounds and common areas.

trust account

A bank account in which money is placed that does not belong to the account owner. Trust accounts are heavily regulated by laws that require specific accounting and that prohibit certain actions or uses of the funds. Generally, funds may not be disbursed from trust accounts until all parties agree. Otherwise, a court will make the determination of the disposition of the money.

turnaround

The successful efforts to reverse the financial downfall of a company.

turnkey

A product or service concept, completely assembled, installed, or set up to begin operation which is then leased or sold to an individual to run as his own venture.

U

UCC search

A search of recorded filings made under the Uniform Commercial Code. Any assets that have encumbrances filed under the UCC cannot be sold or transferred until they are released by the creditor.

unaudited statement

A financial statement, or profit and loss statement, that is prepared from the books and records of the business, but is prepared without independent investigation of the books and records of the business. Lenders may not accept unaudited statements.

undercapitalization

A situation in which a new enterprise starts with too little money to carry it through the beginning stages of development.

unsecured borrowing (debt)

A debt without any real or personal property used as collateral. The loan is granted solely on the strength of the maker's signature.

V

venture capital

Money from investment pools or firms that specialize in financing young companies' growth, usually in return for stock.

venture capital group; or venture capitalist

Investors who provide early financing to new ventures — often technology-based — with an innovative product and the prospect of rapid and profitable growth.

W

waive; waiver

Agreement to set aside a contract term or condition; usually voluntarily, but sometimes based on specific investigation results or other events.

warranty

A promise or pledge that something is what it is claimed to be.

working capital

The amount of funds available to pay short-term expenses. It is determined by subtracting current liabilities from current assets. Working capital can be included in some loan requests.

what ifs

The results of a procedure that examines all the alternatives, upon which actions or reactions may be planned. Often financial spreadsheets are used to calculate the financial impact of alternatives.

win-win

A strategy in business that plans to have all parties to the transaction benefit. If a transaction can be structured as a win-win, all parties will most likely agree to the terms and conditions. The alternate strategy is like a football game — where one must lose for the other to win.

Index

costs and fees, 160

importance of relationship with, 158

knowledgeable, locating, 158-159

lending limits, 159-160

role of, 163t

selection of, 159-160

as source of help, 175

Basis, definition of, 188

Better Business Bureaus (BBBs), as
source of help, 175

BICs (Business Information Centers), as
source of help, 175

Bills of sale

contractual provisions for, 98

definition of, 188

Bodies for Rent Theory, 11

Bookkeeping system, existing, with purchase of ongoing business, 40

Books and records

accurate, importance of, 62

inadequate, in business for sale, 62

misleading nature of, 2, 116

private, definition of, 200

vs. qualitative measures, 2

requests for, in business evaluation, 61

excessive requests, dangers of, 63-64

information to request, 61, 99-100

misrepresentation in, 58, 59, 65

avoiding, 81-82, 115-116

inadvertent, 64

legal recourse, 57, 59, 61

motivating seller to fulfill, 63

offending seller with, 64

withholding of information, reasons for,
61-63, 100

review of

in buying a business, 116

before final sale, 99

transfer of, in contracts of sale, 99-100

Book value, definition of, 70, 189

Bosses, responsibilities of, 10-11

Brokers. *See* Business brokers

Brown out

definition of, 189

sale of business due to, 49

Bulk sales requirements, in contracts of
sale, 99

Bulk sales transfer, 99

definition of, 189

Bureau of the Census, 9

Burnout

definition of, 189

sale of business due to, 49

Business analysis, with purchase of ongoing business, 41

Business brokers

contract with

preprinted, sources for, 182

terms of, 55-56, 161-162

as counselor, 157

credentials, 79, 161

definition of, 189

and deposits

forfeited, 91

holding of, 91

fees and commissions, 79

and inventory, 66
legal obligations of, 57
role of, 161-162, 163*t*
selection of, 54-55, 79, 161
state regulation of, 55
website for, 184

Business entity, selection of type, 109-112, 113*t*

Business ethics, 72, 118

Business forms, source for, 182

Business Information Centers (BICs), as source of help, 175

Business Loan Express, website, 183

Business people, as source of help, 176

Business plans, feedback on, 175

Business schools, as source of help, 176

Business systems, existing, with purchase of ongoing business, 40

Business Week **magazine**, website, 183

Buyer's Broker Representation Agreement, 55
definition of, 189

Buyers of businesses
book value of assets for, 69-70
ignorance of, as area of risk, 116, 117
information requested from
financial statement, 62-63, 103-104
financing information, 63
low offers, wisdom of, 93
optimism of, and sale price, 29, 58-59
thinking like seller, advantages of, 3, 46
training of, as contract prevision, 101-102

Buying a business. *See also* Evaluating a business for purchase; Offers; Selecting a business for purchase
alternatives to, 27-31, 32*t*
danger areas, 116-119, 120*t*
financial health, evaluation of, 56
goals, establishing and evaluating, 54
ongoing businesses, pros and cons of, 35-41, 42*t*
ownership, establishment of, 118
purchase price, allocation of, for tax purposes, 71-72, 95
research, importance of, 53
termination of leases, 67
timing of, 119
unwanted assets, 65
verification and validation of decision, 10-12, 13t
website on, 184

Buy-sell agreement, definition of, 189

C

Capital. *See also* Financing
definition of, 189
evaluation of, 13*t*
insufficient, 10
sale of business due to, 47
and leveraging, wisdom of, 147
loss of, planning for, 21
management of, poor, 10
necessary amount of, 145
raising, advantages of corporations in, 112
risk and, 117

informing of impending sale of business, 85

interviewing, before buying business, 118

list of, as contract supplement, 97

and purchase of ongoing business, 37

Customer base, definition of, 192

D

Debt financing, definition of, 148, 192

Decisions

to purchase, evaluation of, 10-12, 13*t*

responsibility for, 2, 83, 92, 156

Department of Commerce, as information source, 182

Department of Labor, as information source, 182

Deposits

cashing of deposit check, 91-92

definition of, 192

forfeiting of, 90, 91

holding, recommended parties for, 90-91

increases in, 92

size of, 90

Depreciation. *See under* Taxes

Distress

definition of, 192

sale of business due to, 30, 46-48

offers, appropriate, 72, 140

warning signs of, 140

Distribution rights, transfer of, in buying a business, 67

Documents

knowledge of contents, 156

review by legal counsel, 155-156

Dollar per sale, in evaluating a business, 20

Dollar volumes, in evaluating a business, 20

Down time

avoiding, valuation of, 140

definition of, 192

Due diligence, definition of, 193

Due diligence time frame, in contracts of sale, 104-105

E

Earnest money. *See* Deposits

Education. *See* Training and education

Employee(s)

attracting and retaining, 12, 19, 48

hiring

as alternative to selling business, 28

away from competitors, 168

increasing productivity of, 12

indispensable, 16

and sale of business, reaction to, 82-83, 85

trained, with purchase of ongoing business, 39

turnover, reduction of, 12

typical problems with, 11

wages, and employee satisfaction, 12

working as

as alternative to buying, 28

as learning strategy, 168

Enhancement, definition of, 193

Entrepreneur(s)

businesses sold by, as bargain, 49-50

definition of, 36, 193

successful

  characteristics of, 2

  rarity of, 35

Entrepreneur magazine

for location of franchise opportunities, 21-23

website, 183

Entrepreneurship, definition of, 193

Equipment. *See also* Systems; Trade fixtures

cost of

  evaluating, in selecting a business, 20-21

  in ongoing business, 39

expensing of, 71

inventory of, in contract, 93-94

leased, evaluation of leases, 68

specialized, 135

UCC title search on, 67, 68, 116

unwanted, in buying a business, 65

valuation of, 65, 93-94, 139

Equity mortgages, as capital source, 146

Equity partner, definition of, 193

Equity rate of return (ERR) method of business valuation, 138

Escrow, definition of, 193

Estoppels, 117

definition of, 193

Ethics

lack of, in business, 118

and win-win business, 72

Evaluating a business for purchase, 53-72,

73*t*-74*t*. *See also* Selecting a business for purchase; Valuation

financial data, limitations of, 64, 65

information requests

  excessive requests, dangers of, 63-64

  information to request, 61, 99-100

  motivating seller to fulfill, 63

  offending seller with, 64

  withholding of information, reasons for, 61-63, 100

overhead costs, 60

payroll, 60

professional help in

  accountants, 56, 100, 157-158

  appraisers

    for equipment valuation, 65

    for inventory valuation, 66, 97, 139

  attorneys, 56-57

profit and loss statements, construction of, 59-60

rents or mortgages, 60

sales figures, 57-59

  reported vs. unreported, 57, 59

  verification of, 59

sales projections, realistic, 58

sales tax returns, inspection of, 59

seller's reasons for selling, 57 (*See also* Selling a business, reasons for)

Excess over basis, definition of, 72, 193

Expanding a business

and lease vs. purchase decision, 125-126

as motivation for sale, 46

by purchase of other businesses, 41

Expenses, evaluation of, prior to purchase, 56, 99

Expensing. *See under* Taxes

Experience, insufficient, 10, 117

and financing, 168

F

Failure of small businesses

contingency planning for, 21, 54

learning from, 18

rates, by industry, 9*t*

reasons for, 10, 18

Family members. *See also* Spouses

as capital source, 146

contingency planning with, 21

as drain on business, 49

as information source, 178

selling business to, 28

Family problems, sale of business due to, 48-49

Figures. *See* facts and figures

Filing statements, definition of, 194

Finance industry, survival rates of small businesses in, 9*t*

Financial health of business, evaluation of, 56

Financial management rate of return (FMRR) method of business valuation, 138

Financial records. *See* Books and records

Financing. *See also* Capital

availability of, and lease vs. purchase decision, 127

from banks, 148

and experience in field, 168

flexibility in, with purchase of ongoing business, 40

long-term, 145-146

providing information to seller about, 63

from relatives, 146

seller financing, 150-152

definition of, 202

interest rates on, 151

short-term, 145-146

from Small Business Administration, 148-149

of sole proprietorships, 109-110

sources for, 145-152, 153*t*

Fixtures. *See* Furniture and fixtures; Trade fixtures

FMRR (financial management rate of return) method of business valuation, 138

Food service industry, stress in, 47, 48

Forbes magazine, website, 183

Forms, business-related, source for, 182

Fortune magazine, website, 184

Franchises

buying from franchisee, 67

definition of, 194

evaluation of, 22, 23

filing statements

definition of, 194

evaluation of, 22, 23

International Franchise Association, as information source, 183

locating, 21-23
pros and cons of, 35-36
Friends, as information source, 178
Front-end costs, definition of, 194
Furniture and fixtures
definition of, 66, 195
and offer price, 66

G
Goals
alternative methods of achieving, 27-31, 32*t*
changes in, sale of business due to, 49
establishing and evaluating, 30-31, 54
in selling a business, 78, 81
importance of having, 12
verification and validation of, 12, 13*t*
Going public, as capital source, 150
Goodwill
definition of, 195
tax treatment of, 41, 72
in valuation of business, 135
Government Printing Office, as source of
information, 182
Government regulations. *See also* Licenses and permits; Zoning
as area of risk, 117
and equipment costs, 21
satisfaction of, as condition of sale, 117
Grandfather clauses
as area of risk, 118
definition of, 118, 195
Gross rents, definition of, 124, 195
Gut feeling, importance of, 2, 12

H
Happiness, discovering meaning of, 30-31
Help and information, sources of, 173-
178, 182-183
Hobbies, as business idea, 16

I
Improving a purchased business, seller
suggestions for, 101
Imputed interest rate, definition of, 195
Inc. **magazine**, 183
for location of franchise opportunities,
21-23
Income, of small business owner, 10
**Income approach to valuation of small
business**, 133-141, 134-138, 142*t*
using cap rate, 135-136, 137
using cash on cash return, 136, 137
using net operating income, 134-135, 136,
138
using other methods, 138
Indispensable employees, 16
Inexperience, 10, 117
and financing, 168
Information requests, in purchase of
business. *See also* Misrepresentation
buyers' requests
excessive requests, dangers of, 63-64
information to request, 61, 99-100
motivating seller to fulfill, 63
offending seller with, 64

withholding of information, reasons for, 61-63, 100
sellers' requests
    buyer's financial statement, 62-63, 103-104
    buyer's financing information, 63
Information sources, for help, 173-178, 182-183
Institute of Business Appraisers, website, 183
Insurance. *See* also Life insurance
    cost of, prorating in contracts of sale, 98
    small business in
        difficulty of, 47
        survival rates of, 9*t*
Internal rate of return (IRR) method of business valuation, 138
Internal Revenue Service. *See also* Taxes
    as information source, 182
International Franchise Association, as information source, 183
Internet. *See also* Websites
    as information source, 177
    utilization of, 177
Inventory
    appraisal of, in buying a business, 66
    in contracts of sale, 97
    fluctuations in, contractual provisions for, 66
    of included property, in contracts of sale, 93-94
    problems associated with, 19
    unwanted, in buying a business, 65

valuation of, 66, 97, 139
Investment base, definition of, 196
Investment counselors
    definition of, 196
    role of, 161-162
Investments, as alternative to business purchase, 30
Investors, as capital source, 148
IRR (internal rate of return) method of business valuation, 138

J
Joint ventures
    advantages of, 28
    definition of, 196
Journals of trade associations, as source of help, 176

L
Labor Replacement Theory, 10
Lawyers. *See* Attorneys
Lease(s)
    additional rents in, 124
        definition of, 188
    adjoining space, first right of refusal on, 125-126
    assignment of
        in contract of sale, 98
        definition, 196
    backing out of, 128
    copy of, in contract, 95-96
    cost of
        evaluating, in purchase of business, 60

prorating, in contracts of sale, 98
definition of, 196
on equipment, evaluation of, 68
gross rents, 124
  definition of, 195
landlords, evaluation of, 126
negotiation of, 170
noncompete agreements in, 124
options to renew, 124
vs. purchase, 123-129, 130*t*
  affordability, 126-127
  and control of future events, 126
  equity accumulation, 126-127
  from investment perspective, 127-128
  lease rate and terms, 124
    future terms, 125
  and portability of business, 125-126
  purchase, advantages of, 129
  and recovery of investment, 125
  and reversibility, 128
  and sale of business, 128
rate and terms of, 124, 168-169
  future terms, 125, 126
renegotiation of, 118
review of, before purchase, 95-96
subleasing, 128
termination of, in buying a business, 67
transfer of, as area of risk, 118
triple-net leases (NNN), 124
valuation of, 140
Leasehold improvements
  definition of, 66, 67, 196

valuation of, in buying a business, 66-67, 140-141
Legal forms, sources for, 182
Legal sufficiency, definition of, 196
Letter of credit, definition of, 196-197
Leveraging, wisdom of, 147
Liabilities
  assumption of, in contracts of sale, 102
  of corporations, 112
  definition of, 197
  of partnerships, 110, 111
  of sole proprietorships, 110
Libraries, as source of help, 177
Licenses and permits, transfer of
  as area of risk, 117
  as condition of sale, 117
  in contract of sale, 99
  and due diligence period, 104
  grandfathered permits, loss of, 118
Life insurance
  as capital source, 146
  cash value of, definition of, 190
Lifestyle change, sale of business due to, 46
Limited liability companies (LLCs)
  characteristics of, 112
  definition of, 197
Line of credit
  as capital source, 147, 150
  definition of, 197
Liquidated damages provisions
  in contracts of sale, 102
  definition of, 197

Net operating income (NOI)
 calculation of, 134
  preprinted forms for, 182
 definition of, 134, 197-198
 in valuation of business, 134-135, 136, 138
Net proceeds of sale, definition of, 198
Networking, value of, 176-177
Net worth, definition of, 198
New York Times website, as source of information, 177
NNN (triple-net leases), 124
 definition of, 204
NOI. *See* Net operating income
Noncompete agreements, 70, 96
 definition of, 192, 198
 in leases, 124
 overly-restrictive, 96
 tax treatment, 69-70, 96
Nonconforming loan, definition of, 198
Nonconforming use, and loss of permits, 118
Nondisclosure agreement. *See* Confidentiality statements
Nonperforming loan, definition of, 198
Nontransferable, definition of, 198
Notification, definition of, 198

O
Obsolescence, definition of, 198
Offers
 acceptance of, legal requirements for, 187
 conditional, 63-64
 failure to honor, legal recourse for, 104

 format for, 104
 offer price, 56, 58-59
  factors in
   advertising costs, 68
   furniture and fixtures, 66
   inventory fluctuations, 66
   leasehold improvements, 66-67
   patents and rights, 67
   personal property, 67-68
   systems, 68
   trade fixtures, 67
  and information access, 62
  low, wisdom of, 93
  valuation of assets, 68-72
   buyer book value, 69-70
   noncompete agreements, 70
   professional help with, 68-69
   seller book value, 69
  with options, 72
 rejection of, 93, 119
 review by legal professionals, 82
 supporting attachments, 63
 timing of, 119
 verbal, 104
Ongoing business, purchase of, advantages and disadvantages of, 35-41, 42*t*
Operation of business until settlement, 100-101
Overhead
 definition of, 198
 in evaluating a business, 60
 in selecting a business, 19-20

Ownership of business, documentation of, 118

P

Packaging, definition of, 198-199

Parking, insufficient, 168

Partner(s)
as capital source, 147
contingency planning with, 21
and decision to purchase, 13*t*
problems with, sale of business due to, 50
pros and cons of, 110-111, 147
selling business to, 28

Partnerships
buy-sell agreements, 111
characteristics of, 110-111
definition of, 199
partnership agreement, 111

Passive income
definition of, 199
and taxes, 127

Patents and rights
transfer of, in buying a business, 67
valuation of, in buying a business, 67, 135

Payroll taxes, payment of, before sale, 104

Performance mortgages, 40
definition of, 199

Performance notes, 40

Permits. *See* Licenses and permits

Personal property
definition of, 199
inventory of, in contract, 93-94

valuation of, in buying a business, 68, 93-94

Personalty. *See* Personal property

Phone numbers, purchase of, with purchase of ongoing business, 38

Planning for contingencies, importance of, 21

Platform concept, 35
definition of, 199

Portability of business, and lease *vs.* purchase decision, 125-126

Predecessors, mistakes of, 18

Preferred lender, definition of, 200

Price, *vs.* value, 170-171

Pricing
established, with purchase of ongoing business, 38-39
and profitability, 38-39

Professional help. *See* also Accountants; Attorneys; Bankers; Business brokers; Investment counselors
businesspeople as source of, 160
for correction of business problems, 30
in evaluating a business for purchase
accountants, 56, 100, 157-158
appraisers
for equipment evaluation, 65
for inventory evaluation, 66, 97, 139
attorneys, role of, 56-57
importance of, 161
and leases
review of, 96
valuation of, 140

locating, 21-23

market gaps, locating, 17-18

predecessors, learning from, 18

professional help in. *See* Business brokers

sector selection, 19

selection process, 54

  importance of, 15

talent and education, evaluation of, 16

Self-employed individuals

business survival rates, 9*t*

myths about, 8

Seller financing

as capital source, 150-152

definition of, 202

interest rates on, 151

Sellers of businesses

advice on improvements from, 101

asset book value for, 69

"big score" mentality of, 50

ignorance of, as danger to buyer, 116

information provided by, 61

  misrepresentation in, 58, 59, 65

    avoiding, 81-82, 115-116

    inadvertent, 64

    legal recourse, 57, 59, 61

  withholding of, reasons for, 61-63, 100

information requested by

  buyer's financial statement, 62-63, 103-104

  financing information, 63

liabilities, buyer assumption of, 102

operation until settlement by, 100-101

personality of, as asset, 118

rejecting offers, wisdom of, 93

thinking like buyer, advantages of, 3

winning trust of, 63

Selling a business, 77-86, 87*t*

advertising and marketing, 79, 84-86

alternatives to, 27-31, 32*t*, 81

and art of salesmanship, 77

to competitor, 29

confidentiality, 82-83

in distress, 30, 46-48

  definition of, 192

  offers, appropriate, 72, 140

  warning signs of, 140

to family members, 28

final decision, 83

foreign buyers, targeting, 85

goals in, evaluation of, 78

impatience, 83

mechanics of, 83

to partners, 28

professional help in

  accountants, 81-82

  fees and commissions, 80-81

  lawyers, 82

  selection of, 77, 78-81

reasons for, 45-50, 51*t*

sprucing up, 49

timing of, 83, 119

website on, 184

Service clubs, as source of help, 176-177

Service Corp of Retired Executives

valuation of, 93-94

Turnarounds, 167-168
  definition of, 204
Turnkey, definition of, 204
Turnkey theory of business purchase, 65

U
UCC. *See* Universal Commercial Code
Unaudited statements, definition of, 127,
  204
Undercapitalization. *See also* Capital
  definition of, 204
Universal Commercial Code (UCC) title
      searches, on equipment and sys-
      tems, 67, 68, 116
University business schools, as source of
      help, 176
Unsecured borrowing, definition of, 204-
  205

V
Valuation
  of assets, 68-72, 69
    buyer book value, 69-70
    noncompete agreements, 70
    professional help with, 68-69
    seller book value, 69
    taxes and, 69
  of equipment, 65, 93-94, 139
  of inventory, 66, 97, 139
  of leasehold improvements, 66-67, 140-
      141
  of leases, 140
    on equipment, 68

of personal property, 68, 93-94
of small business, 133-141, 142*t*
    for divorce or estate proceedings, 141
    income approach
        using cap rate, 135-136, 137
        using cash on cash return, 136, 137
        using net operating income, 134-135,
            136, 138
        using other methods, 138
    market as final arbiter of, 141
    by market comparisons, 138-139
    by replacement cost, 139-141
    risk and, 141
    subjective nature of, 170
  of startup costs, avoiding, 140
  of systems, 93-94
Value, *vs.* price, 170-171
Venture capital, definition of, 205
Venture capital groups
  as capital source, 150
  definition of, 205

W
Wall Street Journal, website, 184
WAL-MART, impact of, 20
Want ads, and salaries, 11
Warranties and other obligations, disclo-
      sure of, 96
Websites
  for business brokers contract forms, 182
  for business forms, 182
  Business Loan Express, 183
  Business Week magazine, 183

CCIM (Certified Commercial Investment Member) Institute, 182

Census Bureau, 183

Entrepreneur magazine, 183

Forbes magazine, 183

Fortune magazine, 184

Inc. magazine, 183

Institute of Business Appraisers, 183

International Franchise Association, 183

for legal forms, 182

Money magazine, 184

New York Times, 177

NOI calculation sheets, sources for purchasing, 182

S.C.O.R.E. (Service Corp of Retired Executives), 174

Small Business Administration (SBA), 174, 183

Small Business Development Centers (SBDCs), 174

software and publications sources, 182

Streetsmartbooks, 183

Wall Street Journal, 184

Yahoo business site, 183

Wholesale trade, survival rates of small businesses in, 9*t*

Work experience, evaluation of, in selecting a business, 16

Y

Yahoo business website, 183

Yellow pages, and market gaps, 17

Z

Zoning, transfer of
  as area of risk, 116
  as condition of sale, 117
  and due diligence period, 104
  and loss of special zoning, 18

street
smart
books

Thanks for using Small Business Primer. And remember... "Make Your Own Decisions!" Please be sure to give us your feedback on this book by using the Reader Comment formin the back of the book.

Coming soon from

streetsmartbooks

Well, not actually *soon*, but the following subject matters are in the works for future releases. If you have a business subject matter that needs to be written about, contact the publisher: publisher@streeetsmartbooks.com with "book idea" in the subject line. If you would like to be notified when one of the following books are about to be released, put "notify me — (name of book)" in the subject line. Check us out periodically at www.streetsmartbooks.com.

SMALL BUSINESS PRIMER — AGENTS/BROKERS EDITION

A revised edition of the *Small Business Primer* that addresses how to coach and counsel buyers and sellers of businesses. Will highlight the do's and don'ts of business brokerage, how to avoid unnecessary liability, structure the paper trail to keep you out of trouble, and ways to communicate more effectively to buyers and sellers with varying degrees of business acumen. Written for real estate agents, brokers, and business brokers and advisors.

WHEN YOUR BUSINESS FAILS

It happens! Sometimes with warning(s), sometimes at once. How do you get out of a failing business and keep your skin (and maybe some of your assets)? This book will show ways to close your business while avoiding much of the usual liability. It will include cash management problems and solutions, how to find emergency financing, how to pay the little guys and not have the transactions "undone" by the bankruptcy judges. See the difference between Chapter 7, Chapter 11, and Chapter 13 bankruptcies. Find ways to sell your business, even when it is loaded with debt and obligations. Includes reasons businesses fail and tips on how to deal with the IRS. Even how to *avoid* bankruptcy!

THE VALUE OF THE BRICKS TO THE BUSINESS

Should you lease or buy the business property? This book will explore the concepts of cash management and returns on investment to make the decision easier. It's different for every business venture, so there's no pat answer. This book will teach you the concepts on which this decision should be based. Explores the *time value of money* and gives thumbnail formulas to make it easy.

MULTIPLIERS AND FORMULAS FOR BUSINESS INVESTING

What multipliers and formulas exist and how should you use them? Can a formula be trusted for decision-making? Which ones are better and why? How do you calculate them? Is there any easy way to determine value with a minimum of information? What are the best uses for formulas and multipliers? This will not be an exercise in accounting — it will be in the tradition of *streetsmartbooks* — *"Practical books from the trenches."*

UNDERSTANDING THE COMMERCIAL LEASE — FOR THE NONLAWYER.

Certainly your lawyer should review every document you sign — for legal sufficiency and to find areas that do not reflect clear intent. That's the best way to stay out of court. But leases usually have signatures before the lawyer see them. Not good. This book will discuss the type of form you should use, and explain which paragraphs benefit the landlord/owner and which ones benefit the tenant. It starts with who should enter into the lease and winds up on the signature line — who guarantees the lease? In between are hundreds of possibilities. Is a long lease safer than a short one? Is an *option to buy* the same as a *first right of refusal*? Which one is easier to get a landlord/owner to agree to? Why? This book will prove to you that common sense and clear language of intent are the two most critical areas of any lease. This book will include suggested paragraphs for different types of leases.

Visit www.streetsmartbooks.com

Sam Tuttle is available to present his seminars.
For booking, email: publisher@streetsmartbooks.com

ORDER FORM

Please photocopy this form instead of writing in your book.

For discounts on quantity, please email: publisher@streetsmartbooks.com

Quantity	Item Description	$ Each	Total
	Small Business Primer: How to Buy, Sell & Evaluate a Business	$95.00	$95.00
	Shipping and handling per book	$5.00	
		Total	

Method of Payment

❑ Check Enclosed

Please make check payable to: *streetsmartsbooks. LLC* and mail with order form to:
    streetsmartbooks, LLC
    PO Box 2
    Middletown DE, 19709

❑ Please charge my Credit Card the Total amount above

❑ Visa   ❑ MasterCard   ❑ American Express

Name on Credit Card:	
Credit Card Number:	
Expiration Date:	
Signature of Cardholder:	

Shipping Information

Name:	
Company Name:	
Street Address:	
Apt, Suite, Floor. or Dept:	
City / State:	
Zip Code:	
Telephone:	

Reader Comment Form

Please take the time to tell us how you liked *Small Business Primer*
If this book is a library copy, please do not write in it. Photocopy this page instead.

❑ Please respond to my comments or query. My email address is below:

What did you like best about the book?

What could be improved?

Which subjects did you learn most about?

Which subjects could have had more emphasis?

Did you buy the book or borrow it?

What would you like to see added?

Are you planning to buy or sell a business?

Do you feel better prepared after finishing the book?

Please use a separate sheet if more room is needed or if you have additional comments.

Please mail this form to: streetsmartbooks, LLC; PO Box 2; Middletown DE 19709
or fax it to: (302) 378-1487